RELATION ANALYSIS
OF THE FOURTH GOSPEL

A Study in Reader-Response Criticism

Philip B. Harner

MELLEN BIBLICAL PRESS

Library of Congress Cataloging-in-Publication Data

Harner, Philip B.
    Relation analysis of the Fourth Gospel : a study in reader
-response criticism / Philip B. Harner.
        p.   cm.
    Includes bibliographical references and index.
    ISBN 0-7734-2364-8
    1. Bible. N.T. John--Criticism, interpretation, etc. 2. Reader
-response criticism. I. Title.
    BS2615.2.H363   1993
    226.5'06--dc20   93-1708
                                                                        CIP

A CIP catalog record for this book
is available from the British Library.

Copyright © 1993 The Edwin Mellen Press

All rights reserved. For information contact

The Edwin Mellen Press   The Edwin Mellen Press
        Box 450   Box 67
Lewiston, New York   Queenston, Ontario
    USA 14092   CANADA L0S 1L0

                    Edwin Mellen Press, Ltd.
                    Lampeter, Dyfed, Wales
                UNITED KINGDOM SA48 7DY

            Printed in the United States of America

RELATION ANALYSIS
OF THE FOURTH GOSPEL

A Study in Reader-Response Criticism

TABLE OF CONTENTS

PREFACE

The purpose of the present study is to develop the methodology of relation analysis and apply it to the Gospel of John within the context of reader-response criticism. Relation analysis studies the relationships that John presents involving God and people. Reader-response criticism examines the role of the reader in actualizing the meaning of the text. Relation analysis forms the focus, and reader-response criticism provides the setting, for this investigation. The emphasis on relation analysis differentiates this study from others, such as those by Culpepper, McKnight, Moore, and Staley, which are concerned almost exclusively with methodologies of literary theory as they apply to Scripture generally or to the Gospel of John in particular.[1]

Relation analysis seeks to delineate the relationships that John presents among the central *personae* of his narrative, such as God the Father, the Son, the Spirit, believers, and people in general. Within this context it also assesses the role of figures or groups such as Jews, Gentiles, the church, and the world, and it also asks about the function of concepts such as faith, mission, and revelation. In all of these instances relation analysis seeks to identify and correlate the forms of relationship presented in the gospel as a key for understanding John's presentation of Christian faith.

Any methodology must be both extrinsic and intrinsic to its subject matter. It must stand apart and afford a new perspective for analyzing its subject, making it possible to identify aspects of the subject that are not otherwise immediately apparent. At the same time, a method of study must be indigenous to its subject matter, reflecting, as much as possible, the reality of the subject itself rather than imposing norms or concepts from without. If it is to be genuinely helpful, a methodology must be external to its subject matter and at the same time maintain a point of contact with the content of the subject.

The method of relation analysis meets both of these requirements for an effective methodology. It allows the interpreter to take a fresh approach to the gospel, identifying and analyzing relationships among central figures, and then it encourages the interpreter to ask how these relationships, in themselves and in their correlation with one another, form an interpretive framework for understanding the meaning of the subject matter. Ideally, at least, this approach will help the interpreter gain a new perception of structure and content in the gospel.

As a method of study, relation analysis is also internal to the gospel, for John himself emphasizes the significance of the multiple and complex relationships in which his characters stand to one another. Defining these relationships as carefully as possible, he employs them as structural elements giving a sense of unity, balance, and completeness to the gospel. In the Prologue, especially, John calls the reader's attention to the many relationships in which the Word of God stands (e.g., to God the Father, the created world, life, light, humanity, John the Baptist, believers, unbelievers, glory, grace, truth, the law). In this way John not only indicates the importance of relationships for understanding the Prologue, but he also points out major directions that he will follow throughout the remainder of the gospel.

The Table of Contents for this study indicates how the method of relation analysis helps in identifying and understanding significant aspects of John's presentation of Christian faith. The analysis of the relationships among Father, Son, and Spirit helps to clarify John's understanding of the Godhead as the ultimate source of Christian faith. The relationships between God and believers inform the actuality of faith; those between believers and believers provide a basis for the community of faith, and those between believers and the world determine the mission of faith. An analysis of the roles of author and readers, finally, provides insight into the problem of the communication of faith, with special regard to the need for correlating an understanding of revelation with current literary theory. These topics, of course, are not exclusive of one another. In general, each one must presuppose all those that precede. The method of relation analysis provides a fresh approach for investigating John's understanding of each kind of relationship and also the correlations that frequently arise among relationships themselves.

Although it remains in touch with historical-critical methodologies, relation analysis itself is synchronic rather than diachronic. It is concerned to analyze the text as it stands rather than investigate the stages of development through which the underlying materials passed until they reached their final form. Relation analysis can complement other types of literary interpretation. Some of these emphasize the intention of the author in writing the text, some regard the text as an independent entity with meanings and values of its own, and some stress the role of the reader in interpreting the meaning of the text or even creating meaning through the act of reading. Without arbitrarily rejecting values that may inhere in other approaches, this study reflects a special concern for identifying the role of the reader. It seeks to correlate relation analysis with reader-response criticism, a methodology that arose in the 1960's as a way of focusing on the activity of the reader in "actualizing" a text or bringing it to completion.

Relation analysis complements reader-response criticism because both are interested in the "world" or reality to which the reader responds. Relation analysis seeks to identify the network of relationships that John has delineated in the text of his gospel. From the standpoint of reader-response criticism, these relationships constitute the "story world" or "narrative world" that the reader is invited to affirm. A creative tension develops between this narrative world and the reader. On the one hand, the reader may "actualize" the text of the gospel by choosing to accept the values and beliefs inherent in the various forms of relationship involving God and people. In this respect the reader has genuine freedom of decision. On the other hand, the narrative world of relationships gives structure to the direction that the reader's response must take. In this respect the reader is not a completely autonomous self, free to discover any meaning at all in the text.

Reader-response critics emphasize the importance of avoiding the "referential fallacy," which would assume that the narrative world depicted in the text coincides with the actual world of the author or the reader. In the case of the Gospel of John, avoiding this fallacy would mean recognizing that the rich world of relationships that John depicts did not necessarily exist in the actual world of Jesus, the world of John himself, or the world of the reader. John is not attempting to make these claims. He does wish to affirm, however, that the relationships themselves are real in principle, from God's side, and they become real from the human side as people affirm them and commit themselves to them. In this sense John is writing with the intention of inviting his readers to enter into these relationships and bring them to completion.

Although reader-response critics use a variety of terms, some are especially helpful in the present study. The name John, for instance, can refer to the "real author," the person or school of writers and editors who actually produced the Gospel of John. More importantly in the present context, the name John can also designate the "implied author," the aspect of the real author that comes to expression in a literary work and is responsible for the specific ideology -- the values, beliefs, or concerns -- within that work. The real author corresponds to the "real reader," the actual person who picks up a text and reads it. The implied author corresponds in part to the "implied reader," who is presupposed by the text as the reader who fills in the gaps in its narrative, rounds out its presentation of characters, and accepts its ideology. As the term is understood here, the implied reader is not entirely a function of the text, for the implied reader also represents the role that the real reader is called on to fulfill in entering into engagement with the text and bringing it to completion.[2]

It is possible to follow a number of procedures in analyzing a text in terms of reader-response criticism.[3] With regard to the Fourth Gospel, in particular, these procedures involve identification of significant features of the narrative world that John constructs as cues to stimulate the response of the reader. Thus the reader may, for example, seek to do the following:

1) Identify the patterns of relationship, and the correlation of relationships, that John depicts in his narrative world, with special attention

to the questions whom they involve, how they come into being, and what they mean. Relation analysis at this point merges with reader-response criticism by depicting the specific narrative world to which readers are asked to respond. Readers, that is, may "actualize" the text by accepting for themselves the relationships that the narrative world depicts.

2) Identify other aspects of the narrative or the text that may serve as analogies for the role of the reader in "actualizing" the text. These aspects help to establish direction for the activity of the reader in construing meaning in the text. The concept of revelation in history, for example, suggests that the relation of the Holy Spirit to the earthly ministry of Jesus provides a paradigm for the relation of the reader to the text of the gospel, for in each instance the interpretive function is controlled by a historical "given," a *datum* of meaning.

3) Identify differences or tensions that John establishes between the narrative world that he is presenting and the actual world of Jesus, John himself, or the reader. These differences or tensions prompt the reader to engage in critical reflection as a basis for assessing and affirming the narrative world of the text.

4) In contrast to the procedure above, identify parallels or similarities between the narrative world and the actual world. In their own way, such similarities also help the reader to reflect and decide concerning the meaning of the text. They remind the reader that the narrative world is not a theological abstraction but a reality that has significant points of contact with the empirical world.

5) Identify "gaps," as Iser describes them, in the flow of narrative or the presentation of characters in the text. These "gaps" prompt the reader to reflect, make connections, and discern relationships. They suggest significant directions in which the reader may proceed in actualizing the text. As Iser comments, "Thus whenever the flow is interrupted and we are led off in unexpected directions, the opportunity is given to us to bring into play our own faculty for establishing connections -- for filling in the gaps left by the text itself."[4]

6) Identify John's use of paradox as a stimulus for encouraging the reader to reflect on the specific nature of the narrative world that John is depicting and then ask how it can be related to the reader's own world.

7) Identify the types of response, positive or negative, that people make to Jesus within the narrative, and analyze the reasons for these responses and the consequences that ensue. In his analysis of the Fourth Gospel, Culpepper has argued that the plot "is propelled by conflict between belief and unbelief as responses to Jesus."[5] Such responses provide a range of models for the reader to consider in coming to terms with the text.

These strategies for reading all reflect an appreciation of the critical function of the reader in actualizing or completing a text. "It is in the reader," Iser remarks, "that the text comes to life."[6] At the same time, these strategies also reflect the assumption that the author can employ a number of literary devices to indicate the direction in which the reader can respond to the text. The final chapter of this study will explore more fully the relationships among author, text, and reader, with special attention to the significance of the theological concept of revelation in history.

Scriptural quotations in this study are from the New Revised Standard Version of the Bible, copyright 1989 by the Division of Christian Education of the National Council of the Churches of Christ in the USA.

I would like to thank Heidelberg College for granting a sabbatical leave in the fall of 1992 which provided the opportunity to complete this study. I would also like to thank the Reverend Michael P. Moore and Dr. Frank R. Kramer for their kindness in taking the time to review a preliminary draft of this study. Any errors or shortcomings must remain my own responsibility.

Philip B. Harner
Department of Religion
Heidelberg College

CHAPTER I

Father, Son, and Spirit: The Source of Faith

A. The Word and God

The methodology of relation analysis calls attention to the fact that John wishes to think of the Word and God in terms, paradoxically, of both relationship and identity. At the very beginning of his gospel John presents an apparent contradiction: "In the beginning was the Word, and the Word was with God, and the Word was God" (1:1). It is not immediately clear how John can say that the Word was with God and the Word was God. The first assertion describes a relationship, and the second speaks in terms of identity. The fact that John speaks first of relationship, and then of identity, suggests that he is thinking primarily in terms of defining relationships as he begins his Prologue (1:1-18). The fact that he continues to think in terms of relationship in the following verse ("He was in the beginning with God," 1:2) confirms this impression. At the same time, however, it is also important to notice that John does speak in terms of identity between the Word and God. Having indicated that his thought is moving primarily in the direction of defining relationships, John also wishes to make clear that the Word is not other than God.

There is thus a mystery about the Word and God, in that John can speak of them in terms of both relationship and identity. By way of contrast, the question may be raised whether John would speak of people and God in this same way. Would he assert, that is, that people stand in relationship to God and at the same time somehow share in the divine nature? It is important to recall in this connection that John always speaks of people as "children" (*tekna*) of God, and Jesus alone as "Son" (*huios*). This usage indicates that John thinks of Jesus or the Word in ways that would not apply to people generally. The "mystery" of combining relationship and identity seems to be unique to the "persons" of the Godhead.

Through this mystery John indicates to the reader that he is depicting a special "world" which he will invite the reader to affirm and enter. Because it has its basis in the reality of the Godhead, in which relationship and identity can be combined, this world differs from the ordinary world of human experience. John, in effect, challenges the reader to "actualize" the text by perceiving the difference between these two worlds and then affirming the special world that John delineates as a world that has a reality of its own and yet is not unrelated to the world of human experience.

In 1:1-5, in which he focuses attention on the Word, John seems to suggest that the Word can serve as a source of faith precisely because of the paradox that the Word can be described in terms of relationship to God and identity with God. If the Word were only related to God, without at the same time being God, it might make possible only a secondary or inferior kind of faith that would not derive from the revelation of the Father in the Son. If the Word were identical with God, without at the same time being distinct and thus able to stand in relationship to God, the question would arise whether God the Father could reveal himself through the incarnation of the Son. But, as it is, the paradoxical circumstance of the relationship of the Word to God and the identity of the Word with God means that faith has its ultimate basis in, and is made possible by, God himself as he reveals himself through the incarnate Word.

It is also significant, as an indication of the structure of his thought, that John employs the verb "was" (*ēn*) in three distinct ways in 1:1. He uses it to express existence ("in the beginning was the Word"), relationship ("the Word was with God"), and essence ("the Word was God"). John does not formally assign priorities among these three or define their status with regard to one another. Yet it is suggestive that he speaks of relationship in the same context as the attributes of existence and essence. In this way John seems to affirm that the attribute of relationship is just as central as the other two. If the concept of "Word" is to be understood, it must be seen in light of the relationships in which the Word stands as well as in its existence and its essence. Indeed, John may even suggest that the three attributes are so closely conjoined that the existence or essence of the Word can not be fully understood apart from the relationship of the Word to God.

Throughout the remainder of the Prologue (1:1-18), John continues to explicate the various relationships in which the Word stands. The Word, for example, is related to the world, as the one through whom the world was made (1:3, 10). The Word is related to John the Baptist, as the one to whom the Baptist bore witness (1:6-8). The word is related to "his own people" as the one rejected by unbelievers (1:11). Positively, the Word is related to "all who received him," as the one in whom some people believed, so that they became "children of God" (1:12). The Word is also related to believers as the source of grace and truth (1:14, 17). Finally, John ends the Prologue on the same note with which he began, describing the relationship between the Word and the Father: the only Son is not only with the Father but has made him known (1:18). Throughout the Prologue, John's consistent interest in explicating relationships confirms the impression that the theme of relationship establishes the interpretive context in which other concepts, such as existence or essence, are to be understood.

In the texture of John's thought it is also significant that one relationship gives meaning to others. John begins the Prologue by delineating the relationship between the Word and God (1:1). As important as this relationship is in itself, John does not, as it were, let it stand alone. He immediately associates this fundamental relationship with others that the Word receives, with the implication that the Word in its relationship to God, rather than simply the Word in itself, enters into its other relationships with the world, John the Baptist, believers, etc. Throughout the Prologue it would seem that John has in mind the relationship of the Word to God as this relationship underlies and gives meaning to others.

This emphasis on relationships confirms the impression that John is especially interested in depicting relationships in the very first verse of the

Prologue (1:1). Although he does, indeed, speak of existence and essence, he seems to be especially interested in the relationships in which the Word stands -- to God the Father, first of all, and then to the world and to people. In the language of reader-response criticism, John invites the reader to enter a narrative world that gives special attention to relationships (especially that between the Word and God) as the primary source for understanding the meaning of Christian faith and life. John invites the reader to recognize the primacy of relationships in undertaking the process of analyzing the structure of faith and in identifying the content of Christian faith itself. In this way process anticipates content, leading to it and ultimately merging with it because both derive their primary meaning from the relationships that John so carefully presents.

B. Jesus as Son, Son of God, and Son of Man

John speaks of Jesus as Son, Son of God, and Son of man, implying in each case that these titles will be helpful as Christians seek to acquire a fuller understanding of the one in whom they believe. In each case the question may be raised concerning the origin of the title, its usage in earlier Christian writings, and any modification that John made in his own usage. In the context of historical-critical study, these issues are very important in their own right. The methodology of relation analysis, however, seeks to go a step further by asking how John relates these terms to one another and how he employs them in communicating his understanding of Jesus' relationship to God the Father and to believers.

Having introduced the figure of John the Baptist in the Prologue, John continues, immediately afterward, by developing the theme of the Baptist's testimony to Jesus (1:19 ff.). As part of this testimony, the Baptist affirms that Jesus is the "Son of God" (1:34). In the Old Testament this designation could refer simply to David or the Davidic king (II Sam. 7:14; Pss. 2:7; 89:26-27). Nathanael, a little later, may have this idea in mind when he addresses Jesus as the "Son of God... the King of Israel" (1:49). In 1:34, however, John must be using the title "Son of God" as a continuation of his statements in the Prologue concerning Jesus as the Word. The Word was

with God and was God (1:1), and the Word became incarnate as the only
Son and made known the Father (1:14, 18). Now, on the scene of human
history, the Baptist has recognized and testified to Jesus as the Son of God
(1:34). At this point, therefore, John must be using the title in its full
Christological sense: it is Jesus the incarnate Word who is the Son of God.

As he did in the Prologue, John now indicates once again that one
relationship can underlie and inform another. Jesus is the Son of God, the
only Son from the Father; he is also "the Lamb of God who takes away the
sin of the world" (1:29). His role as Son must be seen in connection with his
work as Lamb, a designation which occurs both before and after the Baptist's
confession that Jesus is the Son of God (1:29, 36). As Son, that is, Jesus does
not simply remain content with his relationship to the Father. As Son, rather,
he initiates a new relationship with people in the world, carrying out on their
behalf the function of the Lamb who takes away sin. Jesus' relationship with
the Father, John suggests, does not remain as a static entity but finds
expression in his redemptive relationship with people.[7] In this way John
wishes to remind the reader, in particular, that he is constructing a special
narrative world in which relationships, by virtue of their active qualities, can
be correlated with one another and can reach out beyond themselves to
establish new polarities. As he continues with his gospel account and
introduces new forms of relationships, John evidently wants the reader to be
cognizant of these aspects of the relationships involving God, the Son, and
the world.

Throughout this passage it is interesting to note also that John is
thinking in terms of Father, Son, and Spirit, even though he does not try to
define the relationship of the Spirit to the other two "persons." John the
Baptist testifies that he saw the Spirit descend on Jesus and remain on him
(1:32-33), indicating that he was able in this way to recognize Jesus as the
Son of God (1:33-34). The Spirit thus has a revelatory function in making
Jesus known to the Baptist. The Spirit also functions as the means by which
Jesus himself will baptize (1:33). By emphasizing that the Spirit "remained"
on Jesus, John makes it clear that Jesus, as the Son of God, received the
permanent gift of the Spirit, in contrast to temporary charismatic figures such
as the Judges in the Old Testament. Through these references to the Spirit,

which are the first in his gospel, John suggests that the relation of the Son to the Spirit will be permanent -- somewhat, perhaps, as the relation of the Son to the Father has been permanent. John suggests also that the work of the Son will always be consonant with the work of the Spirit, and *vice versa*. In these ways John seeks to make a beginning, however inchoate it may be, in understanding the function of the Spirit.

In addition to referring to Jesus as the Son of God, John speaks of him as the Son or the Son of man. His usage raises the question whether he regards all three terms as similar or identical in meaning, at least as he uses them with respect to the relationship between Jesus and God the Father.

It is interesting to note, first of all, that most occurrences of the terms Son, Son of God, and Son of man appear in the first twelve chapters of the gospel -- i.e., as part of the account of Jesus' public ministry. Through this usage John wishes to emphasize that those who would learn about Jesus and develop faith in him must perceive that he is indeed the Son. Whoever else he may be, Jesus is the Son who came from the Father, and his relationship to the Father is lived out in the ministry that he renders. Because of this unique relationship to the father, Jesus is the unique person that he is, and he can undertake the unique ministry of word and deed that he accomplishes. John uses all three terms of sonship to express and reinforce this perception of the significance of Jesus' public ministry for those whom Jesus originally encountered and for those readers whom he encounters later through the medium of the written gospel.

The expressions Son and Son of God would clearly appear to have the same meaning for John, in the sense that to speak of Jesus as the Son is to speak of him as Son of God, and Son of God, in turn, must mean more than Davidic king or Davidic messiah. The phrase Son of man may derive ultimately from some different source, as this is represented, for example, in Ezekiel, Daniel, or the Parables (chs. 37-71) of I Enoch. From the standpoint of relation analysis, the important question is whether John uses Son of man in the same way as the other terms.

In this respect it is significant that John uses all three terms to refer to Jesus during his earthly ministry, not only in a general sense but in ways that are closely parallel to each other. As Son, for example, Jesus is the incarnate

Word who has made known the Father (1:14, 18). He is the Son whom God loved and sent into the world (3:16-17; cf. 3:35; 5:20). He is the Son who does the work of the Father (5:19), has life in himself (5:26), sets people free (8:36), and is glorified through his death (17:1).

As the Son of God, Jesus has roles that are similar or parallel to those that he has simply as Son. He is recognized as Son of God by John the Baptist and by Nathanael (1:34, 49). He is the Son of God who frees from condemnation (3:18), speaks words of life (5:25), is glorified through the raising of Lazarus (11:4), and fulfills through his earthly ministry the hope for the coming of the messiah (11:27; 20:31).

As the Son of man, finally, Jesus carries out functions that are comparable to those he performs when he is designated as Son or Son of God. In his role as the Son of man, he descends from heaven and reveals heavenly reality (3:12-13), executes judgment (5:27), bestows life (6:27, 53), and is "lifted up" and glorified in death and resurrection (3:14; 8:28; 12:23, 34; 13:31). In all these ways John uses the terms Son, Son of God, and Son of man to refer to Jesus during his life and ministry on earth.

The further fact that John uses similar or identical language to describe Jesus as Son, Son of God, or Son of man confirms that he is using these terms with virtually the same significance, regardless of differences that they may have had in origin or background. John speaks of Jesus, for example, as the only (*monogenēs*) Son (1:18; 3:16) and also as the only (*monogenēs*) Son of God (3:18). He emphasizes the importance of "believing" in Jesus as Son (3:16, 36; 6:40), as Son of God (11:27; 20:31), and as Son of man (3:14; 9:35). Similarly, John stresses that believers look to Jesus as the one who bestows the gift of eternal life, whether Jesus is described as Son (3:16; 5:21, 26; 6:40), Son of God (5:25; 11:27; 20:31), or Son of man (3:14; 6:27, 53). John presents Jesus as the one who executes judgment, as Son (5:22) or as Son of man (5:27). In a similar way John speaks of Jesus as the one who is to be glorified, as Son (17:1), as Son of God (11:4), or as Son of man (12:23; 13:31).

By using these terms in the same contexts or with the same range of meanings, John evidently wants the reader to perceive that Jesus, in the final analysis, defines the meaning of the terms rather than *vice versa*. The reader does not simply study the background of terms such as Son of God or Son of man and then ask how this background helps in understanding the meaning of Jesus' person and ministry in the Fourth Gospel. This procedure may be an important preliminary step in analyzing the presentation of Jesus in the gospel. At a deeper level, however, it is Jesus who defines or redefines the meaning of any designation that may be applied to him. By being the person that he was and carrying out the ministry that he rendered, he brought out the true meaning of terms such as Son, Son of God, and Son of man. Relation analysis helps to make it clear that John, by using all three terms with reference to the earthly ministry of Jesus, and with virtually the same range of meanings, wishes to indicate that the reader must understand them as Jesus himself gave them meaning.

Several examples will illustrate how Jesus, in John's view, defined the full meaning of these terms, rather than *vice versa*. In 1:49, for instance, Nathanael addresses Jesus as "Son of God... King of Israel." Since Son of God could be used in the Old Testament as a designation for the Davidic king, it appears to fit very well here with the affirmation that Jesus is king of Israel. At this point Nathanael, who is just being introduced to Jesus, probably understands Jesus in terms of the current Jewish hope for the coming of a political messiah who will free the people from their oppressors and reestablish an independent Jewish state (for this kind of hope cf. Psalms of Solomon 17:23-51). At the same time, John wants the reader to understand that he is using these terms in a specifically Christocentric sense, as Jesus himself has given them meaning. Jesus is the Son of God as the only Son who has come from the Father (1:14, 18), and he is King with a kingship that is not of this world (18:36). Only in these ways can he be truly perceived as Son of God and King. Through this literary device of double meaning, John shows how Jesus himself redefines terms and brings out their true significance.

In a similar way John links the term Christ (Messiah) with the designation Son of God (11:27; 20:31). Again, in terms of current Jewish expectations, both expressions could refer to a political messiah who would restore the Jewish state. In this sense it is understandable that Messiah would be linked with Son of God, rather than with Son or Son of man.

Again, however, it is clear that John can use these designations for Jesus only because their current political meanings do not apply to him. Jesus himself, through his ministry of service, has transformed their meaning. He redefines the meaning of messiahship by becoming the non-political Messiah who ultimately gives his life for the world. In this sense, John suggests, Jesus has brought out the true meaning of messiahship, and only in this sense can believers regard him as Messiah.

The description of Jesus as the Son of man who must be "lifted up" (3:14; 8:28; 12:34) provides a third example of John's view that Jesus himself redefined the meaning of current terms. John does not speak of Jesus as Son or Son of God in this connection-only as Son of man. The idea of being "lifted up" is probably a complex image including the events of crucifixion, resurrection, and ascension, as these become stages of one continuous upward movement by which Jesus goes to the Father in heaven. It is specifically as Son of man that Jesus must be lifted up. Yet in Jewish thought, at least as it is represented in the Parables of I Enoch, the Son of man is depicted as a supernatural figure who will come from heaven to earth to preside over the events at the end of the age. This transcendent Son of man would not undergo crucifixion and resurrection. Yet, John indicates, Jesus both fulfilled and redefined the role of the Son of man as he came from the Father, carried out his ministry, and then was "lifted up" through death and resurrection to return to the Father.

It might seem that John is engaged in a process of circular reasoning, describing Jesus as Son of God or Son of man and then indicating that Jesus in effect redefined the meaning of these terms. In this respect it is very possible that the brief designation "Son" enjoys a certain hermeneutical priority in comparison with the other two expressions. In the Prologue to his gospel, John delineates the various relationships in which the Word stands to the Father, the world, humanity, etc. Then John brings the Prologue to a close by a summary assertion describing the incarnate Word as "the only Son" (1:18). This meaning of "Son," as delineated in the Prologue, may well continue to govern further occurrences throughout the gospel. In particular, it may underlie the usage of the longer expressions Son of God and Son of man, facilitating John's endeavor of redefining the connotations of these phrases in light of Jesus' actual life and ministry.

From the standpoint of reader-response criticism, the question arises what John wishes to communicate to the reader through his treatment of the terms Son, Son of God, and Son of man. By indicating that these terms do not define Jesus so much as Jesus defines them, John wishes to suggest that a historical-critical approach, as important as it is, points beyond itself to the narrative world that John is presenting to the reader. In this world the emphasis falls, not on the pre-history of titles, but on Jesus as the one who gives new meaning to titles through the ministry that he conducts and the relationships that he lives out. John invites the reader to perceive, and respond to, this narrative world in which Jesus is the one who redefines the meaning of titles. John also wants the reader to be aware that this narrative world is not an abstraction but is always in contact with the empirical world of human life, in which Jesus conducted his earthly ministry. As D. Moody Smith has recently commented, "It is the genius of the Fourth Evangelist to have created a gospel in which Jesus as the representative of the world above visits and really lives in this world without depriving it of its verisimilitude and without depriving life here of its seriousness."[8]

C. Jesus as Lord

In 1:23, as part of the testimony of John the Baptist, John gives an approximate quotation of Is. 40:3: "I am the voice of one crying out in the wilderness, 'Make straight the way of the Lord.'" For Isaiah, the term Lord referred to Yahweh, or God the Father. John applies it now to Jesus, recalling in this way the close relationship between the Word and God that he has just depicted so carefully in the Prologue. The use of Lord as a designation for Jesus further emphasizes the mystery of the relation between the Son and the Father, who are distinct "persons" yet share the same being. At this point John also reflects the outlook of synoptic tradition, which quoted Is. 40:3 with reference to Jesus (Mk. 1:3; Matt. 3:3; Lk. 3:4). The unique aspect of John's usage is that this application of Lord to Jesus occurs against the background of the relationship between the Word and God delineated in the Prologue. Jesus was not another "lord" of Gentile religious cults nor was he simply a person through whom Yahweh, the God of the Old Testament, was working in a special way. Jesus was Lord as the incarnate Word, who had been with God from the beginning and, indeed, was God. Only against this background of relationship and identity, John implies, can the use of Lord as an appellation for Jesus be fully understood.

John's quotation of Is. 40:3 is also important because it helps to introduce the earthly ministry of Jesus. John the Baptist, after denying that he himself is the Christ, Elijah, or the prophet, now asserts his positive role as the one who is to prepare "the way of the Lord." In the remainder of the chapter the Baptist sees Jesus and testifies to him; Jesus, for his part, gathers several disciples and prepares to begin his public ministry. The designation of Jesus as Lord in 1:23 facilitates the transition from the rather abstract affirmations of the Prologue to the narrative of Jesus' earthly ministry, and at the same time it helps to mark the beginning of the public ministry itself.

As John gives structure to his narrative, it is important to see how 1:23 is related to 12:38. In 12:38, John gives an approximate quotation from Is. 53:1: "Lord, who has believed our message, and to whom has the arm of the Lord been revealed?" The use of "Lord" at this point corresponds in several ways to that in 1:23. As 1:23 quoted from the book of Isaiah (40:3), so 12:38 quotes again from Isaiah (53:1). As 1:23 helped to introduce the public ministry of Jesus, so 12:38 now helps to bring this ministry to a close. Jesus has withdrawn from public activity at this point (12:36b), and from now on he will confine his teachings and actions to the circle of his followers (chs. 13 ff.). Most significantly, 1:23 and 12:38 are the only two Old Testament quotations in the entire gospel in which John transfers the meaning of the word "Lord" from God the Father to Jesus. Serving as they do to enclose the public ministry of Jesus, the quotations reflect John's conviction that God the Father was truly present and active in the ministry of the Son. In spite of this ministry's apparent lack of success (12:37), Jesus conducted it as Lord, giving expression to the theological mystery that the Son shared in the being of God the Father throughout his life on earth as well as his existence in heaven.

The method of relation analysis helps the modern reader identify significant stages in the presentation of John's thought concerning the Father and the Son. In the Prologue, John used terms such as Word and Son to delineate, as precisely as possible, the relation between the Father and the Son. Then John used two Old Testament quotations to provide the framework for his account of the public ministry of Jesus. These quotations both used the term Lord -- originally with reference to God the Father and now with reference to Jesus -- as a way of indicating that the Father was truly present in the ministry of the Son, in spite of the apparent failure of that ministry. These two quotations, in turn, seem to point forward to the confession of Thomas, "My Lord and my God!" (20:28). This confession, as John intended it, may well represent the climax of the entire gospel. It focuses once again on the mystery of the relationship between the Father and the Son, since the terms Lord and God could apply to either one separately, and are applied here to the Son in light of the Son's relation to the Father. The Prologue and the Old Testament quotations in 1:23 and 12:38 have all prepared the way for this culminating confession of faith.

Throughout his gospel, John uses the word Lord (*kurios*) in a way which frequently illustrates the insight of reader-response criticism that meaning depends, at least in part, on the viewpoint of the listener within the narrative or the reader standing outside the narrative itself. Thus the meaning of *kurios* in any passage will depend to a great extent on the way the translator (as reader-interpreter) understands it. As translators are aware, it is very possible also that John sometimes uses the word on more than one level of meaning.

According to the New Revised Standard Version, which may serve as an example at this point, John used *kurios* most often in the sense of "Lord," applied directly to Jesus.[9] Examples of this usage occur in several types of material -- the public ministry of Jesus (in the first twelve chapters), the Last Supper and Farewell Discourses (chs. 13-16), and the accounts of the resurrection appearances of Jesus (chs. 20-21). Through this pattern of distribution John wishes to show that Jesus was truly Lord in all the significant moments of his life on earth, whether he was bringing life to the world, instructing his followers, or reassuring them that he was indeed the living Lord who would ascend to the Father. As John has reminded the reader by his quotations from Isaiah in 1:23 and 12:38, to speak of Jesus as

Lord, *kurios*, is to affirm the authenticity of the presence of the Father in the ministry of the Son, and at the same time to encounter the mystery of the relationship between the Son and the Father. John invites the reader to enter into this world of linguistic usage and share this affirmation of faith along with its attendant mystery.

In a few other passages the New Revised Standard Version translates *kurios* as "sir" rather than "Lord," evidently understanding the word in its attenuated, everyday sense rather than as an expression of Christian faith. In one passage, which is especially illustrative, the meaning of *kurios* changes from one sense to the other, as the man who had been cured of blindness now acquires faith in Jesus:

> Jesus heard that they had driven him out, and when he found him, he said, "Do you believe in the Son of Man?" He answered, "And who is he, sir (*kurie*)? Tell me, so that I may believe in him." Jesus said to him, "You have seen him, and the one speaking with you is he." He said, "Lord (*kurie*), I believe." And he worshipped him. (9:35-38)

Before the man believed, he addressed Jesus as "sir." After he believed, he addressed Jesus as "Lord." Recognizing the play on words, the translators added a footnote explaining that "sir" and "Lord" represent the same Greek word. In a similar way, *kurios* is applied to Jesus in the sense of "sir" in 4:11, 15, 19, 49; 5:7; 6:34. In all these instances, "sir" is preferable as a translation because the speakers within the narrative are not at this point expressing faith in Jesus. Yet John knows that the person being addressed is none other than the Lord, and he assumes that Christian readers will read the narrative in light of their own faith in Jesus as Lord. In this sense the word *kurios*, as applied to Jesus, must have overtones that go beyond the everyday meaning of "sir." On the part of the author, the double meaning is intentional; on the part of the readers, the meaning of *kurios* depends, at least in part, on the interpretive context informed by their Christian faith.

D. Jesus as Divine Healer

John relates in Chapter 5 that Jesus heals a man at the pool of Bethzatha in Jerusalem and then explains his action to some Jews who object to his healing on the sabbath. The fact that Jesus is addressing Jews could suggest that the chapter is concerned with the relationship between Christian faith and the world. From the standpoint of relation analysis, however, the main theme of the chapter is the relationship between the Son and the Father. As the chapter develops, it focuses more and more on the nature and significance of the "equality" that the Son has with the Father, and the long discourse in the second part of the chapter becomes a Christian midrash on the theme of equality. Christian believers, John suggests, must first have some understanding of this theme before they can take the further step of articulating it to the world.

In Jerusalem, at the pool of Bethzatha, Jesus heals a man who had been ill for 38 years, telling him to stand, take up his mat, and walk (5:1-9). The Jews criticize the man for doing "work" by carrying his mat on the sabbath (5:10), and later they also criticize Jesus for his action of healing on the sabbath (5:15-16). Jesus' reply to this charge evidently reflects his reinterpretation of the explanation of sabbath rest in the Old Testament: "So God blessed the seventh day and hallowed it, because on it God rested (*shabat*) from all the work that he had done in creation" (Gen. 2:3; cf. Ex. 31:12-17). Evidently understanding the present work of redemption in terms of a new act of creation, Jesus asserts, "My Father is still working, and I also am working" (5:17). Jesus reflects a view similar to that of Philo, who believed that God does not observe the sabbath rest but "never ceases making."[10] The Jews are offended all the more by Jesus' declaration, understanding it to mean that Jesus is "making himself equal to God" (5:18).

As he develops this narrative, John presents five distinct themes: 1) by carrying his mat, the man is doing work on the sabbath; 2) by healing, Jesus is also doing work on the sabbath; 3) God the Father, in contrast to the Old Testament account, continues to work, even on the sabbath; 4) Jesus, as Son, works on the sabbath, presumably because his role as Son both allows and requires him to work as the Father works; 5) by speaking of God as his Father in this context, Jesus is making himself equal to God.

John seems to regard these five themes in terms of increasing importance for the Christian understanding of the Son in relationship to the Father. The first two themes represent the kinds of ideas that are familiar from synoptic tradition, as Jesus or his disciples perform "work" on the sabbath and thus come into conflict with scribes or Pharisees (e.g., Mk. 2:23-3:6). Without minimizing the significance of these themes, John wishes to place them within a broader framework suggested by the third, fourth, and fifth themes. In particular, as he develops the remainder of the chapter, he shows a special interest in the fifth theme, which concerns the relationship between the Son and the Father.

John himself clearly seems to accept the affirmation that Jesus is "equal to God" (5:18). He considers it very important, however, to specify as accurately as possible how Jesus is equal to God and what meaning this equality has for the earthly ministry that Jesus renders. By itself, the mere assertion of equality could constitute an offense to monotheism, leading to the kind of reaction that the Jews have exhibited (5:18). For this reason John devotes the remainder of the chapter to a discourse in which Jesus, in effect, describes salient aspects of the equality that the Son is privileged to have with the Father.

In the discourse John touches on a number of themes depicting the nature and effect of this equality between Son and Father. The Son, for example, can do nothing of his own accord, but only what he sees the Father doing (5:19; cf. 5:30). Whatever the Father does, the Son does likewise (5:19). The Father loves the Son, shows the Son all that he himself is doing, and will show the Son even greater works (5:20). As the Father raises the dead and gives them life, so also the Son gives life to whom he will (5:21). The Father has given all judgment to the Son (5:22; cf. 5:27). The person who does not honor the Son does not honor the Father who sent him (5:23). The person who hears the word of the Son and believes the Father who sent him has eternal life (5:24). As the Father has life in himself, so he has granted the Son to have life in himself (5:26). The Son seeks not his own will but the will of the Father who sent him (5:30). The works of the Son, which the Father granted him to accomplish, bear him witness that the Father has sent him (5:36). The Father who sent the Son has himself borne witness to the Son (5:37). The Son has come in the name of the Father (5:43).

John does not develop these individual themes because he is more concerned at this point to present them as significant aspects of the equality between the Son and the Father. In their totality they serve to create an accurate impression of the nature and scope of this equality, showing especially how it expresses itself in relationships involving the Father and the Son, and the Son and believers. With reference especially to the relationship between the Father and the Son, John suggests that this equality has a number of characteristics: it is reciprocal, proportional, dynamic, voluntary, outgoing, and perfect.

The relationship is reciprocal in the sense that each party makes the same kind of active contribution to sustain it: the Father loves the Son, and in a very similar way the Son seeks the will of the Father; the Father has borne witness to the Son, and the Son has come in the name of the Father. The relationship is proportional in the sense that the Son acts as the Father acts: as the Father has life and gives life, so also the Son has life and gives life. The relationship is dynamic in the sense that it involves, not simply the status of equality, but actions that presuppose and express this equality. Thus John uses a series of active verbs in depicting the relationship between the Son and the Father -- e.g., does, loves, shows, gives, has, seeks.

The relationship between the Son and the Father is voluntary because each "person" acts freely, without being subject to internal or external constraint. The Son, for example, does not undertake an independent course of action, but chooses to do only what he sees the Father doing; his commitment to this choice means that he "can" do nothing of his own accord. In a similar way the Father shows the Son all that he himself is doing, and he will even show him greater works. The relationship is outgoing in the sense that it points beyond itself and expresses itself in a redemptive concern for the well-being of people, even to the point of offering eternal life to those who believe. The equality between Son and Father, finally, is already perfect. It does not represent a preliminary stage of relationship which will be completed at some later point. The Son is already equal to the Father and by virtue of this equality renders his ministry to the world.

In delineating these characteristics of the relation between the Son and the Father, John emphasizes to his readers that the Son was equal to the Father in very significant ways during his lifetime on earth. Whatever attributes he may have given up when he came to earth, the Son retained this equality with the Father throughout his earthly ministry. It was, that is, as the Son who was equal to the Father, and not as some lesser being, that Jesus brought redemption to the world. Just as John wants his readers to perceive that Jesus conducted his earthly ministry as "Lord," so he wants to emphasize here that Jesus brought redemption as the Son who was expressing his relationship of equality with the Father.

The fact that John discusses the theme of equality in connection with a healing that Jesus performs may perhaps be understood as an elaboration of the perspective of synoptic tradition. In the synoptic point of view, the healings or exorcisms that Jesus performed were presented as signs of the kingdom of God, or concrete demonstrations of the reality of the kingdom already working in human life. "But if it is by the Spirit of God that I cast out demons," Jesus explained, "then the kingdom of God has come to you" (Matt. 12:28; cf. Lk. 11:20). John would probably not wish to deny this connection between Jesus' healings and the coming of the kingdom. He does wish, however, to focus attention on Jesus himself as the one who brings the kingdom. He wishes to emphasize, in effect, that the one who brings the kingdom can be no less than the Son who is equal to the Father. Because John is so concerned to delineate relationships, he shifts the focus of the healing narrative from Jesus as the one who brings the kingdom to Jesus as the Son who is giving expression to a relationship of equality with the Father.

By developing this theme of equality in connection with a healing narrative, John is presenting, in Iser's terms, a "gap" that the reader must fill. It is one thing to write that Jesus healed a man; it is something else to present Jesus as the Son who is equal to the Father. The first does not necessarily lead to the second. Yet John affirms both points, expecting the reader to make the connection by perceiving, in terms of Christian faith, that Jesus' act of healing is nothing less than an expression of his role as the Son who is equal to the Father. In the narrative world that he constructs, John invites the reader to share this understanding of healing as an event that gives expression to the relationship between the Father and the Son.

E. Jesus as Light of the World

Chapters 7 and 8 in the gospel form a unit describing the visit that Jesus made to Jerusalem at the time of the festival of Tabernacles.[11] After some hesitation, in which he makes it clear that he would not make such a visit simply to seek publicity (7:3-9), Jesus goes to Jerusalem (7:10, a private journey that may, as Barrett suggests, recall Mark's theme of intentional concealment[12]). Here Jesus engages in discussions that center on the question whether or not he comes from God. In Jerusalem he also gives pronouncements that parallel the Jewish rites of drawing water and lighting lamps at the festival of Tabernacles: Jesus himself is the true source of living water (7:37-39), and he alone is the light of the world (8:12).

From the standpoint of relation analysis it is important to note that John develops the themes of this visit to Jerusalem within the context of a careful delineation of the relationships among Father, Son, and Spirit. He does, it is true, focus on the role of Jesus at the festival of Tabernacles, and he highlights the contrast between the spiritual realities that Jesus embodies and those represented in the Jewish festival. Yet John never presents Jesus in isolation, as it were, apart from the other members of the Godhead. John is concerned throughout to depict Jesus in the context of his relationships to the Father and the Spirit.

In delineating this context, John focuses here on the role and actions of Jesus in relation to God the Father. He indicates, for example, that Jesus is sent by the Father (7:16, 28, 29, 33; 8:16, 17, 26, 29, 42) and comes from the Father (7:29; 8:42). Jesus does not speak or act on his own authority (7:17-18; 8:28), and he has not come of his own accord (7:28; 8:42). His teaching is not his own, but the Father's (7:16; 8:26, 28, 38, 40). Similarly, his judgment is true because it is his and the Father's (8:16). Jesus knows the Father (7:29; 8:55), seeks the glory of the Father (7:18), does what is pleasing to the Father

(8:29), honors the Father (8:49), and keeps the word of the Father (8:55). Jesus, finally, will soon return to the Father (7:33).

In these ways John depicts the relationship between Son and Father from the side, as it were, of the Son. He undoubtedly emphasizes this point of view because his narrative focuses on the activities of the Son. This focus can be understood, ultimately, as a reflection of John's commitment to the concept of revelation in history, according to which the Son comes to the world, lives a human life, and reveals the Father to people on earth. At the same time, John occasionally presents the relationship from the side of the Father. Thus he indicates that the Father testifies on behalf of the Son (8:18), the Father is with the Son (8:29), and the Father seeks the glory of the Son (8:50, 54). These observations must reflect a conviction on John's part that the relationship between Son and Father is not static or unilateral; it must be seen as dynamic and reciprocal, involving active participation by both parties.

Although John focuses in these chapters on the relationship between Jesus and the Father, he does indicate also that there is a close connection between the completed work of Jesus and the gift of the Spirit. When Jesus is "glorified" through death and resurrection (7:39; cf. 12:23-24), the Spirit will come to believers in a specifically Christian sense (cf. 16:7; 20: 22- 23). The Spirit is depicted here in the imagery of "rivers of living water" that will flow out of the "heart" of the believer (7:38). An alternate translation, according to the punctuation that is assumed for the verse, is that the Spirit would come from the "heart" of Jesus himself. Either way of understanding the verse could represent John's meaning: the divine life is made available to believers through the ministry, death, and resurrection of Jesus, and it is given so abundantly that it wells up within believers themselves (cf. 4:14). The relationship between the Son and the Spirit, John suggests, is reciprocal. The work of the Son, as a completed whole, forms the indispensable condition for the coming of the Spirit, and the bestowal of the Spirit signifies the continuing gift to believers of the eternal life that the Son, as the incarnate Word, brought to the world (cf. 1:4, 14).

Relation analysis of Chapters 7 and 8 helps to identify the coincidence of perspective, intention, and action between the Son and the Father. In a similar way it points to the coordination of events involving the Son and the Spirit. These relationships provide an interpretive context for Jesus' proclamation, "I am the light of the world. Whoever follows me will never walk in darkness but will have the light of life" (8:12; cf. 9:5). These words do not simply refer to Jesus alone, as important as they are in this respect. They also describe Jesus as the Son who stands in relationship to the Father and the Spirit and carries out his work in coordination with the roles of the Father and the Spirit. Only in the context of these relationships can the significance of Jesus' status as the light of the world be fully appreciated.

The method of relation analysis occasionally raises the question of the connection between one relationship and another. In this case it points to the fact that the relationship between the Son and the Spirit, stated concisely in 7:37-39, is presented within the broader context of numerous references throughout Chapters 7 and 8 to the relationship between the Son and the Father. The question arises, therefore, why John would wish to embed one relationship so clearly within the context of another.

By this arrangement John evidently wished to establish very careful hermeneutical control over his presentation of the gift of the Spirit. Just as the coming of the Spirit rests on the completed work of the Son (7:37-39), so the role of the Spirit, in its broadest aspects, reflects the harmony of perspective and purpose between the Son and the Father (Chapters 7 and 8). The gift of the Spirit to believers makes possible the continuing appropriation of the spiritual realities offered by the Son in his relationship to the Father. If this point should be expressed negatively, it would be that the Spirit would not bestow gifts or prompt believers to engage in actions that would be inconsistent in any way with the completed work of the Son or the total relationship between the Son and the Father. John guards against this kind of misunderstanding by making the gift of the Spirit dependent on the glorification of the Son and then placing this affirmation within the broader setting of the relation of the Son to the Father.

John's conviction that the gift of the Spirit can not be understood apart from its context in the relationships involving Spirit, Son, and Father sheds light on an interesting textual variation in 14:26. This verse refers especially to the didactic function of the Spirit after Jesus has returned to the

Father: "But the Advocate, the Holy Spirit, whom the Father will send in my name, will teach you everything, and remind you of all that I have said to you." The last part of the verse contains a definite relative clause with its verb in the indicative (*eipon*, "I have said"). It indicates that the role of the Spirit will be to remind believers of the teachings that Jesus gave during his earthly ministry and help them understand the meaning of these teachings for their own time. Just as it was in 7:37-39, the role of the Spirit here is dependent on the completed work of Jesus.

A variant reading for the last part of 14:26 introduces a distinctly different idea. This reading has an indefinite relative clause, "whatever I may say to you" (*an eipō*, in Codex Bezae and some other manuscripts). This variant reading would diminish the importance of the earthly ministry of Jesus by suggesting that Jesus, as risen Lord, continues to give new teachings through the Spirit. It is conceivable that these new teachings could extend, modify, or even contradict the ones that Jesus gave during his earthly ministry. The variant reading, that is, points in the direction of the idea of "continuing revelation," *revelatio continua*. Although the variant reading can be rejected on the grounds of insufficient textual support, it is interesting that the method of relation analysis would also provide a reason for rejecting this particular variant and the idea of continuing revelation that it introduces.

John's view of the role of the Spirit also has implications for the role of the reader who seeks to find meaning in the process of reading the text. For John, the role of the Spirit is closely connected with the work of Jesus during his earthly ministry. The Spirit functions as interpreter by helping believers understand the meaning of Jesus' actions and teachings. The Spirit takes account of these actions and teachings as something "given," a primary datum of divine revelation in history. Although the Spirit also helps believers understand the continuing significance of Jesus' earthly ministry, it never loses its relation to this ministry itself. John's view of the relation of the Spirit to historical revelation would suggest that the reader has an analogous relation to the written text of the gospel. Although the reader seeks to construe meaning in the process of reading the text, the reader would also respect the integrity of the text as a religious and literary datum and would seek to maintain a relationship of continuing dialogue with the text. In this way the relation of the Spirit to the earthly ministry of Jesus establishes a significant direction for the activity of the reader in entering into engagement with the text.

F. Public Ministry and Final Hours

The Gospel of John, like Jesus' robe itself, often seems to be seamless because the parts fit together so smoothly. If the gospel does have a major seam, it would be at Chapter 12, which marks the transition from Jesus' public ministry to his final words in private with his disciples. By various devices, including the motif of the relationship of the Father and the Son, John uses Chapter 12 as a link between Chapters 11 and 13. More broadly, he uses Chapter 12 to connect the two major periods of Jesus' earthly life -- his public ministry and his final hours with his disciples.

In Chapter 11, John relates that Jesus restored Lazarus to life as the final, climactic sign of his public ministry. It is interesting that John gives no indication how the disciples, Mary and Martha, or even Lazarus responded to this event. Since he is concluding his account of Jesus' public ministry, John evidently wishes to focus on the response of the Jews who witnessed the occurrence. As they have often done in the past, the Jews give a divided response to Jesus, some believing and others reacting negatively (11:45-46). The decision of the Jewish authorities to put Jesus to death (11:53) brings to a culmination the previous instances in which Jewish opponents sought to persecute Jesus (5:16-18; 7:1, 19, 25, 30, 32, 44; 8:37, 40, 59; 10:31, 39), just as Jesus' own action of restoring Lazarus to life brings to a climax the signs that he has performed in the course of his public ministry. The pattern of divine sign and divided response, John suggests, is characteristic of the entire period of Jesus' public ministry.

John links Chapter 11 with Chapter 12 by the proleptic note in 11:2 identifying Mary as the person who anointed the feet of Jesus; the actual anointing is related later, in 12:3. The mention of Martha and Lazarus in these scenes also strengthens the link between Chapters 11 and 12. On the other hand, John connects Chapter 12 with Chapter 13 by emphasizing the relation between the Father and Jesus: the Father sent Jesus into the world

(12:44-45), and now, at the beginning of the Last Supper, Jesus knows that it is time to return to the Father (13:1, 3). In these ways John utilizes Chapter 12 to mark the transition from Jesus' public ministry to the final hours that Jesus spent with the disciples. At the same time, John establishes connections between Chapters 11 and 12, and between 12 and 13, to help the reader perceive the continuity between these two major periods of Jesus' earthly life.

From the standpoint of relation analysis, it is significant that the relation between the Father and the Son provides the essential basis for this continuity that extends from Chapter 11 through Chapter 13. When he raises Lazarus from the dead, Jesus declares that the ultimate purpose to be discerned in the illness of Lazarus is to glorify both the Father and the Son (11:4); the two are so closely related that glorifying one coincides with glorifying the other. In a similar way, Jesus expresses his conviction that the Father always hears the Son (11:42). He accepts the anointing of his feet by Mary as a proleptic anointing for burial (12:7). Then, as the anointed king of Israel, he enters the city of Jerusalem (12:12-15), in contrast to the sequence of events in Mark (11:1-10; 14:3-9) and Matthew (21:1-11; 26:6-13), in which the "triumphal entry" precedes the anointing for burial. Jesus receives the inquiry from some Greeks (12:20-26) as an indication that the world-wide scope of his ministry has, in principle, been established. At this point he can speak, therefore, of his departure from the world, expressing once more his confidence in God as his Father (12:27-30). As he begins the Last Supper with the disciples, he continues to express this theme of confidence in his heavenly Father (13:1-3).

The relation between the Father and the Son is especially prominent in Jesus' words at the close of Chapter 12. The exact setting of this passage (12:44-50) is not clear, since Jesus had apparently concluded his public teaching at 12:36b or possibly even 11:54. In itself, the passage does not seem to be restricted only to the disciples. Even though he does not give it a specific setting or audience, John may have inserted it at this point as a summary of important themes that Jesus has presented in his public teaching, such as believing, seeing, light, darkness, salvation, judgment, and eternal life. Binding all these themes together, and giving unity to the passage as a whole, is the relationship between the Father and the Son: to believe in the Son is to believe in the Father (12:44), to see the Son is to see the Father (12:45), to hear the Son is to hear the words that the Father has commanded him to speak (12:49-50). In its pivotal location at the close of Chapter 12, the passage reflects John's special interest in utilizing the motif of the relation of the Father to the Son as an essential connecting link in the transition from Chapter 11 to Chapter 13.

The question arises what function this motif has in Chapters 11 through 13. Why, that is, does John refer so consistently to the relation between the Father and the Son as he makes the transition from Jesus' public ministry to the events of his last hours? Throughout his gospel, of course, John is concerned to present the Father-Son relationship. The specific question here is what significance he finds in it at this point, since he refers to it so often and seems to highlight its importance.

One reason why it is so important for John to present the relationship at this point is that it shows the Father's continuing presence with the Son. God does not support Jesus throughout his public ministry, for example, and then desert him afterward, when Jesus is facing the final hours of his life on earth. By emphasizing that the relationship between the Father and the Son endures, John can anticipate Jesus' later affirmations of this relationship, such as Jesus' words about the Father in 14:7-11, his prayer to the Father in 17:1-26, his use of the divine self-predication in 18:5, and his confidence of ascending to the Father in 20:17. Because the relationship of Father and Son does continue as Jesus' public ministry comes to a close, it can endure to the end of his life on earth and express itself in his return to the Father in heaven.

Another reason why John is so careful to articulate this relationship in Chapters 11 through 13 is that he wishes to show that it underlies and governs the Christological understanding of Jesus himself throughout the entire course of his life on earth. The Messiah who performed signs and gave teachings was also the Lamb of God who gave his life for the world; the crucified Savior who died for others was also the historical person, Jesus of Nazareth, who lived and worked on earth. It would be a mistake, John implies, for Christian faith to focus its interest exclusively on one aspect or the other of Jesus' person and work, or on one period or the other of his life on earth. Overemphasizing the significance of his deeds and teachings could result in an inadequate appreciation of the importance of his death, and *vice versa*. The relationship of the Father and the Son governed the entire course of Jesus' life, and everything that Jesus accomplished reflected the way that he chose, with the support of the Father, to give voluntary expression to this relationship.

From the standpoint of reader-response criticism, it is significant also that John presents a narrative world in which relationships endure. The Father remains with the Son at all times -- including the moments of rejection during his public ministry, and during the apparent failure of his final hours. John invites the reader to reflect on this world in which relationships endure and can be trusted. The reader may find that the empirical world is both different and similar-different, because its own relationships are not perfect, and similar, because its relationships do function, however imperfectly. John, in effect, encourages the reader to actualize the text by correlating the narrative world of enduring relationships with the polarities of dissimilarity and similarity characteristic of the relationships experienced in the reader's everyday world.

A final reason why John emphasizes the Father-Son relationship in Chapters 11 through 13 is that an awareness of the continuity of this relationship helps the reader adjust to the noticeably slower pace of narrative time in the concluding chapters of the gospel. In terms of the Nestle Greek text, John devotes some 43 pages to Chapters 1-12, which depict a period of several years in Jesus' life on earth. Then he gives 23 pages -- about half as many -- to Chapters 13-21, which describe the final hours of Jesus' life and then the resurrection appearances. Because the flow of narrative time is much slower now, the reader needs some sense of continuity with the earlier parts of the gospel and some theological rationale for the slower pace of narration. The reader's awareness that the Father-Son relationship governs the entire gospel aids in making this transition to the new narrative circumstances of the concluding chapters.

G. The Father's Love for the Son

Perhaps more than any other theme in his gospel, John treats the concept of love in a wide variety of settings and relationships. He speaks, for example, of the love involving the Father and the Son within the Godhead itself, the love involving God and believers, and the love that believers are to show to one another. These three dimensions of love reflect, respectively, John's thought concerning the source of faith, the actuality of faith, and the community of faith. Each dimension of love, by its very nature, involves relationships between a subject who loves and an object who is loved. Each aspect of love, furthermore, is related to the following aspect: as the Father has loved the Son, so the Son has loved the disciples (15:9); as the Son has loved the disciples, so they are to love one another (13:34). Thus John treats the theme of love, not only in terms of relationships, but in terms of the correlation and proportionality of these relationships with one another.

John uses two verbs (*agapaō, phileō*) and a noun (*agapē*) in treating the theme of love. It is important to recognize that he employs these word-stems synonymously, whatever dimension or aspect of love he is describing. This is particularly the case with regard to the two verbs. When John indicates that the Father loves the Son, he can use either *agapaō* (3:35; 10:17; 15:9; 17: 23-24, 26) or *phileō* (5:20). When he notes that Jesus loved Lazarus, he combines *agapaō* (11:5) with *phileō* (11:3, 36). When he speaks of "the disciple whom Jesus loved," he uses *agapaō* (13:23; 19:26) and *phileō* (20:2). When he writes of the Father's love for believers, he can use both *agapaō* (14:21, 23; 17:23) and *phileō* (16:27). Whatever subject-object pattern he is describing, John gives no indication that he is thinking in terms of any difference in meaning between the two verbs. Although he uses *agapaō* much more often than *phileō*, he clearly regards the two as synonymous.

One of the most important verses in which John speaks of the Father's love for the Son is 3:35: "The Father loves the Son and has placed all things in his hands." The present tense, "loves," suggests that this relationship of the Father to the Son is a universally valid, continuing relationship. John's comment elsewhere, that the Father loved the Son before the foundation of the world (17:24), confirms the idea that the relationship of love is eternal:

the Father always loves the Son, apart from time and within any period of time. It would be impossible, John implies, to think of the relationship in any other way.

By emphasizing that the Father loves the Son (3:35), John complements his earlier statement in the Prologue that the Word "was in the beginning with God" (1:2) -- i.e., has always been with God from eternity. Whereas the Prologue spoke of an eternal relationship between the Father and the Son, John now speaks more specifically of an eternal relationship of love. This relationship, furthermore, is reciprocal, since John indicates elsewhere that the Son also loves the Father (14:31). Although John does not speak very often of the Son's love for the Father, it is significant that he associates this love with the Son's obedience to the Father: "I do as the Father has commanded me," Jesus explains, "so that the world may know that I love the Father" (14:31). Even in the case of the Son, John indicates, love can express itself through obedience.

There is a close parallel in content and structure between 3:35 ("The Father loves the Son and has placed all things in his hands") and the familiar declaration in 3:16 ("For God so loved the world that he gave his only Son..."). In both instances, God's love is portrayed as a dynamic love that expresses itself in some specific action on behalf of its object. In 3:16, God so "loved" that he "gave." In 3:35, God "loves" and "has placed" (literally, "has given"). Although the tenses differ, the verbs for "love" (*agapaō*) and "give" or "place" (*didōmi*) are the same in each case. In each instance, God's love is an active love that expresses itself in the act of giving to the recipient. At the same time that the first relationship (3:35) is parallel to the second (3:16), it also underlies the second -- the Father loves the Son and has given him all things, and then it is precisely this Son whom the Father gave to the world, in order that those who believe in him may have eternal life.

As the Father's relation to the Son involves the act of giving him all things, it also involves the attitude of complete confidence in the Son. Because the Father "has placed all things" in the hands of the Son (3:35), the Son is not only "above" all things (3:31) but actually has power over all things. The Father's love for the Son involves his complete confidence in the Son's use of this power. The Father trusts, in effect, that the Son will exercise this power in ways that are consonant with the reciprocal relationship of love between Father and Son. The dynamic of love, John suggests, involves not only the act of giving, but an attitude of wholehearted trust that accompanies the gift. The Father's trust, John indicates, was not misdirected, since the Son showed his love for the Father by doing the Father's will (14:31).

John's declaration that "The Father loves the Son..." (3:35) occurs in a passage in which he speaks of Jesus as "the one who comes from above" (3:31) and "speaks the words of God" (3:34). John's language at this point is remarkably reminiscent of the gnostic idea of a heavenly redeemer who comes to earth and reveals a special redemptive "truth" (*gnōsis*) to the elect. In gnostic mythology also, as Bultmann has noted, the Father loves the Son, and the Son speaks the words of the Father.[13] The fact that John avoids using the noun *gnōsis* may well be one indication that he wants to distinguish his views from those of gnosticism, in spite of some similarities of terminology. Theologically, it is very possible also that John would wish to differentiate his understanding of Jesus from the gnostic conception of a heavenly redeemer by insisting that Jesus must always be seen within the total context of the relationship of the Father to the Son. This relationship has always existed from eternity, as John has indicated in the Prologue (1:1), and it will continue to govern the incarnation, ministry, death, and resurrection of Jesus. It is only within this context, John suggests, that Jesus can be depicted as the one who comes from above and speaks the words of God.

John's statement in 3:35 that "The Father loves the Son..." is closely connected with the gift of eternal life: "Whoever believes in the Son has eternal life..." (3:36). The Father's love for the Son and his action of placing "all things" in his hands create a situation in which the Son can become the immediate source of eternal life itself for those who believe in him. Without minimizing in any way the significance of the Father as the ultimate source of life, John focuses attention here on Jesus as the Son who is the object of faith and the proximate source of eternal life. Because the relationship of love between the Father and the Son continues to obtain, it underlies and makes possible this focus on the role of the Son.

In a very similar way the affirmation of the Father's love for the Son in 5:20 introduces a passage which leads up to the belief in eternal life. In 5:20, John writes that "The Father loves the Son and shows him all that he himself is doing..." The following verses deal with issues such as resurrection, judgment, and honor. The passage then culminates with Jesus' words in 5:24, "Very truly, I tell you, anyone who hears my word and believes him who sent me has eternal life, and does not come under judgment, but has passed from death to life." The connection between love and eternal life, prominent in 3:35-36, is equally clear in 5:20-24. In both passages the Father's love for the Son, as important as it is, points beyond itself to the gift of eternal life for those who believe.

In both of these passages the Father's love for the Son creates a continuing relationship within which the Son becomes the immediate source of eternal life. John recognizes that the Father is the ultimate source of life, just as the Son is the proximate source (5:21). John does not, however, speak simply of believing in God and receiving eternal life. As he elaborates the structure of Christian faith, he identifies the relation of love between the Father and the Son as the context in which each, in his own way, may be perceived as the source of eternal life. Thus John is thinking in terms of relationships, not only as the context in which an article of faith such as eternal life may be understood, but as part of the content of Christian faith itself.

By emphasizing this relationship between the Father and the Son, John may well imply that relationships are integral to the structure of eternal life. Just as the relation between the Father and the Son establishes the setting in which each becomes the source of life, so the believer who receives eternal life may well find that this gift involves richer relationships with the Father, the Son, and other believers. The quality of eternal life, like the Father's love in which it has its ultimate source, would therefore be active and dynamic, rather than passive or static.

This aspect of eternal life would be consistent with the only passage in which John undertakes to give a definition of this concept: "And this is eternal life, that they may know you, the only true God, and Jesus Christ whom you have sent" (17:3). Although the word "know" may have an intellectual component, its primary meaning here, as often in the Old Testament, would be "to stand in the right relationship with" and even "to acknowledge obligations to" (cf. Am. 3:2; Hos. 2:19-20; 4:2, 6; 6:3, 6; 13:4). For John, too, eternal life is not only knowing about God but being and living in the right relationship with God. It is not unexpected, therefore, that John can speak of eternal life in close parallelism with the idea of salvation (3:16-17).

Throughout his gospel, John states a number of times that the Father loves the Son (3:35; 5:20; 10:17; 15:9; 17:23-24, 26). Sometimes he makes this declaration with specific reference to the Father-Son relationship, and sometimes he states it in connection with other forms of relationship. In most instances John makes no attempt to identify a reason why the Father loves the son. This love, he implies, can have no cause other than itself. The Father loves the Son because it is his nature to do so; he loves because he loves.

Only at one point does John give a reason why the Father loves the Son. Jesus explains, apparently to the Jews, "For this reason the Father loves me, because I lay down my life in order to take it up again" (10:17). Jesus goes on to emphasize the voluntary nature of his self-sacrifice (10:18). Perhaps John would regard this reason, in terms of modern logic, as "sufficient but not necessary." John apparently wishes to call attention to the Father's own acknowledgment of Jesus' voluntary action. Even though the Father's love has, in principle, no cause other than itself, the Father can still love the Son because the Son voluntarily lays down his life for others. This is the kind of love, John suggests, which is intrinsically unmotivated and yet at the same time, paradoxically, can recognize and respond to the actions of its object.

As John describes the love between the Father and the Son, he employs paradox (or apparent paradox) as a literary device for calling the reader's attention to the special nature of the narrative world that he is presenting. It seems to be a paradox, for example, that the Father loves the Son and yet gives him commands; the Son, conversely, expresses his own love for the Father through obedience to these commands. It seems to be a paradox also that the Father, loving the Son, has given all things to him, and yet, loving the world, has given the Son himself to the world. It seems to be a paradox that the Father's love for the Son so readily involves others besides the Son, since this love is so closely connected with the gift of eternal life for those who believe. It seems to be a paradox that relationships can become both the context and the content for this central gift of eternal life. It seems to be a paradox, finally, that the Father's love for the Son has no cause other than itself, yet it also has a basis in the Son's voluntary sacrifice of his life.

It is perhaps a moot point whether these themes represent paradoxes or only apparent paradoxes. In either case, John uses them to call attention to the special qualities of God's love as he is depicting it in his narrative world. In this way he stimulates the reader to compare this narrative world with the "real" world of everyday life and to ask how the Father's love for the Son can be a part of this everyday world.

H. The Supportive Role of the Spirit

John treats the role of the Spirit in so many ways, in the context of so many relationships, that it would be possible to discuss the Spirit in each chapter of the present study. It is appropriate, however, to survey the work of the Spirit at this point, since the Spirit always stands in very close relationship with both the Father and the Son. The Spirit never functions independently, as it were, apart from the context of these relationships. In this sense the Spirit constitutes, along with the Father and the Son, the source of Christian faith.

A survey of the work of the Spirit will suggest, indeed, that John regards the Spirit as having a supportive role rather than an independent function. The Spirit, that is, serves primarily to support and enrich the relationships into which the Father and the Son enter, rather than form separate, self-contained relationships of his own. The Spirit is more interested in strengthening and sustaining the relationships that the Father and the Son have established than in becoming a party to independent relationships of his own. Preferring to work within the context of other relationships, the Spirit assumes in this way a supportive role with regard to the work of the Father and the Son.

John's references to the Spirit in connection with the testimony given by the Baptist illustrate how the Spirit functions to strengthen relationships involving other parties. The Baptist testifies that he saw the Spirit descend and remain on Jesus (1:32), and Jesus, in turn, is designated as the one who will baptize with the Holy Spirit (1:33). The Spirit at this point helps the Baptist recognize Jesus as the one who "ranks ahead" of him (1:30). Having recognized Jesus in this way, the Baptist can then begin his work of testifying to Jesus as "the Son of God" (1:34). John notes also that the Spirit "remained" on Jesus (*menō*, 1:32-33). This use of the verb "remain" or "abide" differentiates Jesus from temporary charismatic leaders, such as the Judges of the Old Testament. More immediately, however, it seems to provide a reason why Jesus himself can baptize with the Holy Spirit. As the one permanently endowed with the Spirit, Jesus can utilize the Spirit in baptism and eventually transmit the Spirit to those in the Christian community (20:22).

From the standpoint of relation analysis it is significant that the Spirit has the function in this passage of helping John the Baptist and then Jesus himself as they conduct their ministries. Although the Spirit enters into relation with the Baptist and with Jesus, these relationships almost immediately point beyond themselves. They clarify and facilitate the Baptist's relation to Jesus, and then Jesus' own relation to his followers. The relationships in which the Spirit is a party, as important as they are, function primarily to support relationships involving other parties.

In a similar way John speaks of the work of the Spirit in connection with spiritual rebirth (3:5-6, 8). Jesus receives a visit from Nicodemus, who seems to represent "orthodox" or "normative" Judaism, especially as it is receptive to learning about Jesus and his teaching. In this passage John uses double meanings as a literary device to indicate definitions or comparisons-to be born "anew" (*anōthen*) is to be born "from above" (*anōthen*, 3:3, 7), i.e., from the Spirit of God that comes down from above; and this "Spirit" (*pneuma*), like the "wind" (*pneuma*), has a reality and motive power of its own that will assuredly achieve results. As a further literary device in this passage, John shifts from singular "you" (3:3, 5, 7-8, 10-11) to plural "you" (3:7, 11-12) to suggest that in Jesus' conversation with Nicodemus, the

Christian church of John's own time is also addressing the contemporary Jewish community. An important characteristic of this passage, finally, is the connection that John makes between "Spirit" and the idea of "being born" (3:5, 6, 8b). The work of the Spirit here is to make possible a spiritual rebirth -- a reorientation of values, beliefs, and commitments; this rebirth, conversely, seems to occur for John only as a result of the operation of the Spirit. From the perspective of these literary strategies, John indicates that Jesus said to Nicodemus, "You must be born from above....So it is with everyone who is born of the Spirit" (3:7-8).

Throughout this passage John is less interested in depicting the relationships in which the Spirit plays a separate part than in describing the supportive function of the Spirit in enabling and enhancing relationships involving other parties. Nicodemus represents the Jews, who need to be "born again" with the help of the Spirit. But then the Jews, in turn, represent all those who do not believe in Jesus. Ultimately, therefore, the Jews represent the world, as the self-contained sphere of human society which lives by its own standards and values instead of placing its faith in Jesus as the Son of God. Thus when Jesus converses with Nicodemus about the need to be born again, he is also, in the final analysis, speaking about the world's need to believe. The Spirit, by helping non-believers make the transition to faith, brings new vitality and hope to the relationship between God and the world: God not only loves the world, but sends the Spirit to help it turn to faith.

John is also thinking in terms of relationships when he comments, "He whom God has sent speaks the words of God, for he gives the Spirit without measure" (3:34). The context describes the work of Jesus as the Son, who comes from heaven (3:31), gives testimony (3:32), speaks the words of God (3:34), receives all things from the Father (3:35), and becomes the source of eternal life for those who believe (3:36). The reference to the Spirit occurs within this passage that focuses on the work of the Son and the relationships involving the Son, the Father, and believers. It is uncertain whether John is thinking of the Father or the Son as the one who "gives the Spirit without measure" (3:34). Yet it is clear that the Spirit supports the work of the Son, helping the Son in speaking authentic words of God or helping believers recognize the Son's words as the words of God. In this way the Spirit helps to facilitate the relationship between the Father and the Son, or the Son and believers, or possibly both.

Some special problems of translation appear in the conversation between Jesus and the woman of Samaria in Chapter 4. It is not always clear, that is, whether the Greek word *pneuma* should be translated as "spirit" or in a more personal sense as "Spirit." As part of his conversation with the woman, Jesus says, "But the hour is coming, and is now here, when the true worshipers will worship the Father in spirit and truth, for the Father seeks such as these to worship him. God is spirit, and those who worship him must worship in spirit and truth" (4:23-24). In these verses the New Revised Standard Version (NRSV) has rendered the word *pneuma* as "spirit" rather than "Spirit." The decision whether or not to capitalize the word in translation is not always easy. It would appear, in general, that the Greek word can be translated as "the Spirit" if it has the definite article. The NRSV often follows this principle (1:32, 33a; 3:6, 8b, 34; 7:39a; 14:17, 26; 15:26; 16:13). Sometimes, however, the NRSV translates the arthrous *pneuma* as "the wind" (3:8a) or "the spirit" (6:63a; 19:30). Usually it translates anarthrous *pneuma* as "spirit" (3:6; 4:23, 24ab; 6:63b; 11:33; 13:21), but sometimes as "Spirit" (1:33b; 3:5; 7:39b; 20:22).

In addressing problems of this kind, translators must not only pay attention to the use or non-use of the definite article, but they must also ask in each instance whether John is specifically thinking of the "Spirit" in a personal sense as part of the Godhead. It can be difficult to decide, for example, whether Jesus baptizes "with holy spirit" or "with the Holy Spirit" (1:33b). Similarly, it is uncertain whether Jesus as risen Lord bestows "holy spirit" or "the Holy Spirit" on his disciples (20:22). It is important to remember that a noun in Greek is not necessarily less individualized or specific just because it lacks the article, since an anarthrous noun may have a qualitative connotation (e.g., "by a Son" in Heb. 1:2 contrasts the nature of God's revelation through his Son with his earlier revelations through the prophets; the phrase emphasizes the qualitative difference between "Son-revelation" and "prophet-revelation"). In the case of 1:33b and 20:22, the presence of the adjective "holy" may reinforce the qualitative sense of the anarthrous *pneuma*, without detracting from its individuation, so that "the Holy Spirit" would be the preferable translation. This is, indeed, the translation that the NRSV gives for these verses.

Some commentators also suggest that it would be mistaken to put too much emphasis on the use or omission of the article with *pneuma*, since the article may not be used consistently.[14] Moule remarks, for example, that "it seems to me rather forced to interpret the anarthrous uses (e.g., in the Gospels) as uniformly meaning something less than *God's Holy Spirit*."[15] Moulton (Turner) suggests that the anarthrous phrase "holy spirit" means "a divine spirit inspiring man," but he also notes that the issue is complicated by the non-use of the article with proper nouns and in prepositional phrases.[16] It would seem to be possible, therefore, that the anarthrous "holy spirit" could refer sometimes to "the Holy Spirit" in a personal sense. Thus the NRSV is very probably correct in rendering anarthrous *pneuma* as (the Holy) Spirit in 1:33b and 20:22.

In the present passage, 4:23-24, it is likely that the NRSV is also correct when it translates anarthrous *pneuma* as "spirit," even though the thought is not without overtones of "the Spirit" in a personal sense. To say that "God is spirit" (4:24) is to think of God as creative energy or life-giving activity (cf. 3:8). It suggests that God is unknown and unknowable, except as he has "spoken" and revealed himself through his Word (cf. 1:18). Since the Spirit, in a personal sense, helps people understand the truth revealed by the Word (14:26; 16:12-15), to speak of God as "spirit" is to foreshadow the work of the Spirit as Paraclete or Helper. Because God is spirit, true worshipers will worship him "in spirit and truth" (4:23-24), i.e., in the life that Christians receive in Christ, who is himself the truth. Here again, anarthrous *pneuma* may be translated simply as "spirit," but in the context of John's thought the term also suggests the activity of the Spirit of God, just as "truth" refers to the revelatory and redemptive work of Christ.

Although *pneuma* in 4:23-24 is primarily "spirit" rather than the "Spirit," it is significant that the concept serves here, as often, to strengthen and enrich other relationships. In this case *pneuma* enhances the relationship between God and believers. By expressing in particular the idea of the new life that believers receive in Christ, *pneuma* gives new meaning to the worship that believers can offer to God. Believers, that is, can come now "in spirit and truth" to worship the God who is himself spirit.

John develops this connection between "spirit" and "life" in his allusions to the bread and wine of the Lord's Supper in Chapter 6: "It is the spirit that gives life; the flesh is useless" (6:63a), and "The Words that I have spoken to you are spirit and life" (6:63b). Although *pneuma* has the definite article in 6:63a, it is translated in the NRSV as "the spirit" rather than "the Spirit." The term "spirit" is contrasted to "flesh" in 6:63a (cf. Is. 31:3), and it is joined with "life" in 6:63b. This usage suggests that "spirit" is used here in a general sense to denote the creative energy or power that comes from God and gives new life to those who believe. Since John is discussing the elements of the Lord's Supper at this point, he wishes to emphasize that it is the life-giving spirit, rather than the bread and wine themselves, that creates "true food" and "true drink" for participants in the sacrament (6:55). John does want to emphasize that revelation takes place within history, and the bread and wine of the Lord's Supper must always have reference to the one who gave his own life "for the life of the world" (6:51). The spirit that gives meaning to the bread and the wine does not operate at random, as it were, without reference to the revelation through the Word in history. Yet John also wishes to emphasize that "it is the spirit that gives life" (6:63), so that participation in the Lord's supper conveys the assurance of receiving the gift of eternal life (6:50-51, 54, 57-58).

At the same time that he points to the death of Jesus as the historical basis for the Lord's Supper, John also indicates that he is viewing the Lord's Supper from the standpoint of the completed work of Jesus, who came from heaven as Son of man and then ascended to heaven once again (6:62). From this stand-point John may well be thinking of the arthrous *pneuma* as "the Spirit," so that "it is the Spirit that gives life' (6:63), just as the Spirit brings about new birth (3:5-8) and can be described as "living water" (7:38). Although Jesus was the bearer of the Holy Spirit during his earthly ministry (1:33), it was only after his death and resurrection that he bestowed this Spirit on his followers (7:39; 20:22). In the final analysis, John suggests, it is not simply "spirit," but "the Spirit" given by the risen Lord, that makes the elements of the Lord's Supper "true food" and "true drink" (6:55). In this sense the translation of *pneuma* reflects John's own perspective as a Christian living in the post-resurrection period and viewing Jesus' earthly ministry as a completed whole.

John may well be thinking of the arthrous *pneuma* in 6:63 in a double sense. It is "the spirit" in contrast to material substance, the creative energy that comes as a life-giving reality from God. At the same time, from the standpoint of the completed work of Jesus, it is also "the Spirit," bestowed by the risen Lord, who specifically gives the promise of eternal life to participants in the Lord's supper. If the meanings of "the spirit" can carry over to enrich the understanding of "the Spirit," then the work of "the Spirit" also illustrates how a rather general religious concept of "spirit" becomes more specific and personal within the context of the historical ministry of Jesus as the Son of man who descended from heaven and then returned to heaven.

In terms of relation analysis, it is significant that the Spirit here, as elsewhere, does not establish new relationships of his own but serves to confirm and complement relationships involving other parties. In this case the Spirit functions primarily to enrich the relation between Jesus and his followers. John calls attention to this role of the Spirit by describing two ways in which Jesus' followers may receive eternal life. They receive this gift by believing in Jesus (6:40, 47; cf. 6:68-69), and they receive the same gift by partaking of the Lord's Supper, with its reference to the body and blood of Jesus (6:50-51, 54, 57-58). John does not wish to describe two distinct forms of Christian life, or two separate ways of reaching the same goal, in case some people would prefer the way of faith and others would choose the sacrament. On the contrary, John wishes to make it clear that these two ways of receiving eternal life overlap within Christian experience, precisely because the Spirit who gives life in the Lord's Supper is the same Spirit bestowed by the risen Lord who gave his own life for the life of the world. Through his life, death, and resurrection, Jesus made it possible for those who believe in him to receive eternal life. The Spirit enriches the relationship between Jesus and believers by bringing it to a special focus in the celebration of the Lord's Supper.

The passage in which Jesus refers to the Spirit in terms of "rivers of living water" (7:38) illustrates once again how the Spirit has the role of strengthening and enriching the relationship between Jesus and his followers. At the festival of Tabernacles in Jerusalem, Jesus exclaimed, "Let anyone who is thirsty come to me, and let the one who believes in me drink. As the scripture has said, 'Out of the believer's heart shall flow rivers of living water'" (7:37b-38). This translation, from the NRSV, reflects the view that Christian believers have received the "living water" so abundantly that it wells up within them. This idea would be consistent with the imagery of 4:14, which depicts "a spring of water gushing up to eternal life" within believers themselves. The Greek text of 7:38 actually speaks of "his heart" rather than "the believer's heart." According to the punctuation that is adopted for the verse, "his heart" could refer to the believer or to Jesus himself. In the latter case, Jesus would be depicted directly as the source of eternal life (cf. 5:21, 26). Either interpretation is possible, and either is comprehensible within the context of John's thought.[17]

Whether the "living water" comes from the heart of the Christian believer or from Jesus himself, it is important to note here that John explicitly connects the gift of eternal life with the gift of the Spirit (7:39). When Jesus has been "glorified" through death, resurrection, and ascension, he will give the Spirit in a special way as the characteristic hallmark of the Christian community. As the risen Lord, on the first Easter evening, he will bestow the Spirit on the disciples (20:22). More generally, the Father will send the Spirit in Jesus' name (14:26), or Jesus will send the Spirit from the Father (15:26) as "Advocate" or "Helper" for the ongoing life of the Christian community. Although John describes the gift of the Spirit in somewhat different ways, he clearly assumes that the coming of the Spirit is dependent on the completion of the earthly ministry of Jesus. In a similar way, he views the coming of the Spirit as an expression of the harmony of redemptive purpose shared by the Son and the Father. For this reason he can say that the Father will send the Spirit (14:26) or Jesus will send the Spirit (15:26).

The different ways in which John views the reception of eternal life illustrate how the Spirit functions to complement the work of Jesus during his earthly ministry and at the same time strengthen the relationship between the risen Lord and his followers in the continuing life of the Christian community. When John speaks of the way people receive eternal life, he usually indicates that they receive this gift by believing in Jesus (3:16, 36; 6:40; cf. 3:15; 5:24, 40; 6:47; 20:31). In his account of the feeding of the 5,000, John suggests that people receive eternal life by participating in the sacrament of the Lord's Supper (6:50-58). When he speaks of the Spirit, John indicates that the metaphor "rivers of living water" has reference to the Spirit, as it will be given to believers after the earthly ministry of Jesus (7:38). John believes, that is, that the gift of the Spirit conveys or confirms the gift of eternal life itself for believers within the Christian community. The coming of the Spirit is dependent on the completion of Jesus' work on earth. At the same time, the Spirit establishes a sense of continuity between Jesus' earthly ministry and the post-resurrection church, so that the life-giving relationship that Jesus offered to his original followers carries over to the relation between the risen Lord and Christian believers of later times.

Although John does not give a formal doctrine of the Trinity, it is significant that he presents the work of the Spirit in ways that presuppose and continue the close relationships among Father, Son, and Spirit. This is the case when he presents the Spirit as the Spirit of truth, who is also, at the same time, the "Advocate" or "Helper" (*paraklētos*, Paraclete). It is the case also when he depicts the Spirit as sent from the Father and from the Son. It is the case, finally, when John speaks of the involvement of the Spirit in human history in a manner that has some parallels to the incarnation of the Son. In all of these instances John thinks of the Spirit as working within relationships involving the Father and the Son rather than breaking away, as it were, to form independent relationships of his own.

When John specifically presents the Spirit as the Spirit of truth, he describes the Spirit at the same time as Advocate or Helper. He uses the two phrases together, for example, in 14:16-17: "And I will ask the Father, and he will give you another Advocate to be with you forever. This is the Spirit of truth..." In a similar way he uses both together in 15:26: "When the Advocate comes, whom I will send to you from the Father, the Spirit of truth who comes from the Father..." In both passages, "Advocate" appears first and then is explained by "the Spirit of truth," which stands in apposition with it. A similar pattern is evident in 16:4-15, in which "Advocate" is mentioned first (16:7), and "the Spirit of truth," as a clear reference to the Advocate, is mentioned a few verses later (16:13). In the Gospel of John, Advocate appears elsewhere only in 14:26, where it is explained by the expression "the Holy Spirit." The phrase "the Spirit of truth" stands in an especially close connection with the word "Advocate," since it occurs in John only in the passages indicated above (14:17; 15:26; 16:13) -- i.e., it never appears by itself, apart from "Advocate."

John's usage suggests that the work of the Spirit in promoting truth is the work of the Spirit as Advocate. The Spirit of truth can not be received by the world, because the world does not know him; but believers know him, because he abides with them and is in them (14:17). The Spirit of truth, or Advocate, testifies on behalf of Jesus (15:26). He proves the world wrong about sin, righteousness, and judgment (16:8-11). He guides believers into all the truth, he speaks whatever he hears, he declares the things that are to come, and he glorifies the Son by taking what is his and declaring it to believers (16:13-15; cf. 14:26). In summary, the Spirit of truth, or Advocate, has the function of helping believers understand the work and significance of Jesus, who is himself the way, the truth, and the life (14:6).

John's own use of the term "Advocate" (*paraklētos*) is consistent with the suggestion of Barrett that the word can best be understood by reference to the meaning of related words such as the verb *parakaleō* and the noun *paraklēsis*. Both of these words, he notes, can refer to Christian preaching or exhortation and also to the consolation or salvation of the messianic age. The meanings come together in that the main purpose of Christian preaching is to bring to people the salvation made available through the work of Jesus.[18] The Spirit is "Advocate" in the sense of promoting these activities within the context of the relationships among the persons of the Godhead -- reminding believers, for example, of all that Jesus said to them (14:26), testifying on behalf of Jesus (15:26), and declaring to believers what Jesus has received from the Father (16:14-15). In ways such as these the Spirit works within his relationships involving the Son and the Father, confirming their intentions and continuing their work in the Christian community.

John continues to think in terms of relationships involving the Father and the Son when he speaks of the "sending" of the Spirit. On the one hand, he indicates that the Father will give or send the Spirit as Advocate (14:16-17, 26). On the other hand, John can also say that the Son will send the Spirit in his role as Advocate (15:26). From the point of view of relation analysis it becomes evident that John's thought is even more complex, since in all these instances he presents the Father and the Son as acting in concert: Jesus will ask the Father, and the Father will give the Spirit (14:16-17); the Father will send the Spirit in the name of the Son (14:26); the Son will send the Spirit from the Father (15:26). Even when the Father or the Son seems to be acting independently, the other is always involved.

When he speaks this way about the sending of the Spirit, John is not trying to present paradoxes simply for their own sake. He is seeking instead to express the harmony of attitude and identity of redemptive purpose that characterize the activities of both the Father and the Son. The relationship between the Father and the Son, John suggests, precludes independent or divergent action on the part of either. The fact that Father and Son can both send the Spirit means that the Spirit represents the expression of the relationship existing between them. John, strictly speaking, does not indicate that the Spirit creates or even enriches this relationship, perhaps because he presupposes that the Spirit has functioned in this way from eternity with regard to a relationship that is already as strong as it could be. In his gospel, John chooses to emphasize that the Spirit gives concrete expression within human history to the relationship between Father and Son, as each shares in the work of salvation.

Parallels between the sending of the Spirit and the sending of the Son suggest that John, once again, is perceiving the work of the Spirit within the context of relationships involving the Father and the Son. The involvement of the Spirit in human history is parallel to the incarnation of the Son in the sense that both occurrences represent divine intervention in history and divine revelation in history. The two occurrences are parallel also in that both involve a degree of self-sacrifice or self-limitation. The Son gave up his position with the Father in heaven to come to earth and assume the limitations of finite human existence; in an analogous way, in terms of relation analysis, the Spirit refrains from emphasizing those relationships in which he would be an independent party and chooses instead to define his role in terms of strengthening and enriching other relationships involving the Father, the Son, and Christian believers.

Along with these parallels between the sending of the Spirit and the sending of the Son it is important, of course, to notice differences. The incarnation of the Son occurred first, and the Spirit comes to the Christian community only after the completion of the earthly ministry of the Son (7:39; 20:22). This sequence is necessary so that the earthly ministry of the Son can provide a *datum* in history which then serves as a continuing referent for the work of the Spirit. The incarnation of the Son lasted for the brief span of a human life, whereas the activity of the Spirit, in John's view, continues indefinitely (14:16). The Son was sent into the world by the Father, as the expression *par excellence* of the Father's redemptive intention toward the world (3:16-17). The Spirit, in contrast, is sent by the Father and the Son, as a reflection of the relationship existing between them and a representation of the harmony of redemptive purpose that they share.

Since the Spirit gives expression within human history to the relation between the Father and the Son, the activity of the Spirit can not be divorced from the work of the Father and the Son. It must, that is, always have reference to the Father's action of sending the Son into the world and the Son's own work of bringing light and life to the world. Here again, John indicates, the Spirit has the function of working within relationships involving the Father and the Son rather than establishing independent relationships of his own.

A special issue arises at this point in the interpretation of the Gospel of John. If John (the real author) had had the opportunity to revise his work one more time, he might possibly have given a fuller, more systematic account of the nature and work of the Holy Spirit, parallel to the presentations that he gives for the Father and the Son. As the text stands, it is necessary for the reader to recognize that John (the implied author) has left gaps in his treatment of the Spirit, pointing to one aspect or another of the Spirit's work but not developing these points into a systematic account or "doctrine" of the Spirit.

Reader-response criticism suggests that the implied author, writing in this way, would want the implied reader, and eventually the real reader, to understand the reason for these gaps. John may well be suggesting that the reason lies in the voluntary self-limitation of the Spirit, so that the Spirit intentionally chooses to focus his own work on strengthening relationships involving the Father and the Son rather than operating independently, as it were, to establish separate relationships of his own. John does not regard the Spirit as less important for this reason. Indeed, he seems to present the self-limitation of the Spirit as a positive aspect of his understanding of the Spirit and a major component of the narrative world that he invites the reader to affirm.

CHAPTER II

God and Believers: The Actuality of Faith

A. Revealing, Believing, Becoming

The focus on the Word of God at the beginning of the gospel provides the context in which John presents his understanding of the act or process by which people enter into relationship with God. The Word, on the one hand, is the source of life and light for "all people" (1:4), and this light enlightens "everyone" (1:9). Those who believe in the Word, on the other hand, receive "power to become children of God" (1:12). The fact that 1:4 and 1:9 are followed by 1:12 means that a specific act of believing is necessary to enter fully into relationship with God. Simply being a person, a part of the created world, is not sufficient for entering into this kind of relationship. Believing in the Word, John indicates, is necessary to receive the light and life that have their source in the Word.

The focus on the Word throughout the Prologue indicates that people enter into relationship with God the Father by believing in the Son. In this respect their relationship with the Father is mediate rather than intrinsic. People receive this relationship by believing in the Son (1:12), who is the source of life and light (1:4, 9) and also of grace and truth (1:14, 16-17). Whatever status people may have as parts of the created world, and whatever knowledge of God they may be capable of acquiring, John affirms that they can become "children of God" only by believing in the Son, the incarnate

Word. Although John does not deny that people have worth as members of the order of creation, or that they may acquire some knowledge of God in this capacity, his interest lies in the critical importance of faith in the incarnate Word as the basis for entering into fullness of relationship with God.

John continues to explore the nature of faith as he begins his presentation of the public ministry of Jesus. When Jesus turned water into wine during the wedding celebration at Cana, he "revealed his glory; and his disciples believed in him" (2:11). John's words here suggest that the one event provided the basis for the other -- i.e., that the revelation of Jesus' glory evoked the disciples' response of believing. In this pattern, revelation of Jesus' glory occurs first, creating the possibility of faith, and then faith follows as a response to divine revelation.

This sequence appears to be different from that in the Prologue, in which John suggested that people believe in Jesus' name (1:12) and thus become children of God (1:12), seeing the glory of Jesus (1:14) and receiving grace (1:16). Believing, in this way, seems to occur first, establishing the condition for the experiences of becoming, seeing, and receiving.

Both sequences, paradoxically, may be integral to the texture of John's thought. God must take the first step, as it were, and reveal something of himself if people are to have any possibility of believing. Thus the Son makes known the Father (1:18), and Jesus reveals his glory (2:11). Then those who believe become children of God (1:12), living continually by God's grace (1:16), and they have the spiritual insight to perceive the glory of the only Son when the Word becomes incarnate and lives a human life (1:14).

This paradox suggests that the believers' relationship to God, as John understands it, is dynamic and active. Believers can have faith in God only because God has first given the revelation to which faith responds. But then this response allows believers to enter a new situation of heightened spiritual perception and ongoing life sustained by God's grace. The believers' relationship with God is less a static condition than a continuing dynamic of responding, believing, and doing. As he begins his treatment of the structure of Christian faith, John wants his readers to be aware of these aspects of relationship with God which constitute an essential part of the narrative world that he presents. The readers can then ask themselves how this relationship is different from, or similar to, the divine-human relationship that they may be familiar with in their experience up to this point in their lives.

B. Obedient Son and Risen Lord

John presents further aspects of Christian faith in the incident in which Jesus "cleansed" the Jerusalem temple by driving away the money changers and vendors (2:13-22). John shares this incident with synoptic tradition (cf. Matt. 21:12-17; Mk. 11:15-19; Lk. 19:45-48). The exact meaning of the event in the Synoptics is uncertain. Jesus may have been protesting against the commercial activities in the temple area, against extortion on the part of the money changers and vendors, against the sacrificial system itself, or (very possibly) against the misuse of a particular area, known as the Court of the Gentiles, which had been set aside for the use of non-Jewish peoples. Whereas the Synoptics place the incident near the end of Jesus' ministry, John puts it near the very beginning. It is possible that John has intentionally located the incident at this point because he regards the themes that it develops as representative of Jesus' ministry in its entirety. John wants to use the incident to delineate important aspects of Christian faith that will be illustrated throughout the course of Jesus' ministry.

From the standpoint of relation analysis, John's account of the cleansing of the temple falls into two parts: the actual "cleansing," with Jesus' reference to the temple as "my Father's house" (2:13-17), and then the ensuing discussion between Jesus and the Jews, with the concluding note that Jesus' disciples remembered his words "after he was raised from the dead" (2:18-22).

The first part of the passage focuses on the relationship between the Son and the Father. By cleansing the temple, Jesus is correcting an abuse and restoring the temple to its proper function. More importantly, he is acting as the Son who represents the interests of the Father and acts on behalf of the Father. His relationship with the Father means, in effect, that he carries out the will of the Father in the world of human life and, specifically at this point, in the world of human religious practice. Referring to the temple as "my Father's house" (2:16, an expression absent from the synoptic accounts), Jesus cleanses it and makes it suitable again to serve its intended purpose.

The second part of this incident deals more directly with the relationship between Jesus and his followers, with special reference to the way in which the followers arrive at understanding and faith. In reply to a question from the Jews, Jesus asserts, "Destroy this temple, and in three days I will raise it up" (2:19). From now on, John suggests, true worship will not take place in the temple in Jerusalem but will occur in the name of the only Son, who rose from the dead that all who believe in him may have eternal life (cf. 4:21-26). The disciples apparently did not understand this at first, but after the resurrection they remembered that Jesus had said this and they believed the scripture and his word (2:22).

This second part of the incident illustrates John's conviction that faith in Jesus is always faith that is formulated in light of Jesus' resurrection. The followers of Jesus can understand the meaning of his earthly ministry and believe in him as the incarnate Son only in light of their faith in him as risen Lord. This backward look through the prism of the resurrection provides the necessary condition and essential perspective for a true understanding of Jesus' earthly ministry.

The method of relation analysis helps the reader perceive that the first part of this incident deals with the relationship between the Son and the Father, and the second part explores an important aspect of the relationship between Jesus and his disciples. At the same time, the reader becomes aware of the literary tension between these two sections of the narrative. The reader perceives a "gap," as Iser would call it, in seeking for a logical connection between the two parts of the narrative. If Jesus cleanses the temple and makes it suitable for worship once again, why would he then speak of his own resurrection as the basis for the new, true worship that takes place in the name of the risen Lord? There would seem to be no reason to restore the Jerusalem temple and then immediately declare it obsolete in comparison to the new center of worship that the followers of Jesus are privileged to have.

It would not be possible to remove this inconsistency with the argument that John wanted to portray the Jerusalem temple as suitable for worship until the time of the resurrection of Jesus, when Christian believers would receive a new basis of worship in the name of the risen Lord. From a strictly historical point of view, John may well have looked at the situation in this way. But he is telling the entire story of the cleansing of the temple from the standpoint of his own resurrection faith, just as he indicates that the disciples themselves understood the incident from the perspective of their resurrection faith. In this way John is also inviting the reader to understand the incident in the light of faith rather than as simply a historical narrative.

In terms of relation analysis, the integrity of the passage derives from the correlation of the two types of relationship that John presents. The first part of the passage deals with the relationship of the Son to the Father -- i.e., Jesus, as Son, acts on behalf of the Father by restoring the temple to its intended use. The second part refers to the relationship of Jesus to his disciples -- i.e., Jesus' words can be understood by the disciples only retrospectively, in light of their faith in him as risen Lord. Although it is inconsistent to restore a temple which immediately becomes obsolete, John evidently allowed this inconsistency to stand because he was interested primarily in the relationships that the passage presented.

John, in particular, wants the reader to perceive the connection between these two relationships. The same Son who was obedient to the Father and represented the interests of the Father was the Son whose resurrection provided a new basis for Christian worship and made possible a new understanding on the part of the disciples. The relationship of Son to Father underlies and informs the relationship of Jesus to his disciples. This is the case, not only in the cleansing of the temple, but also, because of the programmatic position of this incident, throughout Jesus' ministry as a whole. It is always the Son who stands in relationship to the Father who calls upon his disciples to follow him. Conversely, John suggests, to have faith in Jesus as risen Lord always means to recognize him as the Son who carried out the will of the Father during his earthly ministry.

C. Relationship and Concept

The incident concerning Jesus and the Samaritan woman (4:1-42) might seem at first to illustrate the theme of "Believers and the World," since the woman could represent a certain group of people to whom the early Christians brought their gospel. The references in the narrative to harvesting and reaping (4:35-38) indicate that John did indeed wish to point to this aspect of the incident. In terms of historical study, there may be a connection at this point with the account of the apostle Philip, who "went down to the city of Samaria and proclaimed the Messiah to them" (Acts 8:5).

From the point of view of literary structure, the incident concerning the Samaritan woman forms part of a sequence of narratives in which John depicts the expanding scope of Jesus' ministry. First Jesus encounters Nicodemus, a representative of "orthodox" Judaism (3:1-21). Then he meets the Samaritan woman, who represents sectarian Judaism or, more accurately, a group that had broken away from Judaism (4:1-42). Shortly afterward, Jesus heals the son of an official, who is probably Roman and thus stands for the major power of the day. Still later, Jesus will receive an inquiry from some "Greeks," who represent the remainder of the Gentile world (12:20-26). Jesus' ministry is complete now, in the sense that it has reached, in principle, the entire world, both Jews and Gentiles. For this reason, after receiving the inquiry from the Greeks, Jesus immediately begins to speak of the close of his work on earth (12:27 ff.).

It is very likely that John did wish to present this sequence of events illustrating the ever-widening horizons of Jesus' ministry, from "normative" Judaism to the entire world. The narrative concerning the Samaritan woman forms an integral part of this sequence. The method of relation analysis, at the same time, suggests another helpful approach in interpreting this narrative. In speaking with the Samaritan woman, Jesus discusses topics such as living water, eternal life, worship in spirit and truth, and his own identity as Messiah. The passage culminates in the declaration that Jesus "is truly the Savior of the world" (4:42). By focusing on concepts such as these, John indicates that he is concerned to present important aspects of Christian faith within the context of Jesus' conversation with the Samaritan woman. In this respect the woman does not represent, in the first instance, the "world" to which believers bring their message. She stands rather as a model for believers themselves, as they develop faith in Jesus, seek to understand its significance, and share it with other people.

From this point of view the relationship that Jesus establishes with the Samaritan woman becomes a paradigm for the kind of relationship that God seeks to establish with believers. Jesus comes to the woman in her homeland, although Jews did not ordinarily travel through Samaria (4:4-5). He takes the initiative in meeting her and beginning a dialogue (4:7). He reveals life-giving spiritual truths to her, although she is very slow to understand (4:10-26). Finally, the relationship that Jesus has established continues to influence the woman as she returns to her city and bears witness to him (4:28-30, 39).

As John constructs his narrative world, he wants the reader to perceive that Jesus' relationship with the Samaritan woman serves as a model for the relationship that God establishes with believers. God comes to believers, sometimes unexpectedly, in the concrete circumstances of their daily lives. He takes the initiative in making his presence available to them and offering them new possibilities of life in living relationship with himself. He reveals spiritual truths in which they can believe and by which they can live. Finally, he intends that they express this relationship in their own lives by sharing their faith with others, even though their own understanding of their faith may be imperfect.

As John depicts in this way the relationship that God establishes with believers, it is also significant that he introduces theological concepts within the context of relationship. This means, on the one hand, that relationship with God does involve the activity of analyzing and understanding theological concepts. Relationship does not simply exist by itself, without any need on the part of believers to understand the content of their faith. If religion, in modern terms, is existential, it is also conceptual.

John's procedure also means, on the other hand, that theological concepts are not complete in themselves apart from their context in a living relationship with God. If believers are to understand their faith in the fullest way, they must perceive that concepts about God, as important as they are in themselves, point beyond themselves to the relation with God in which believers always seek to live. Thus when John speaks, for example, of eternal life, worship, or Jesus' role as Messiah (4:7-30), he is pointing to the need for appreciating the importance of these concepts, and, at the same time, he is placing them within the context of the living relationship with God in which believers can most fully appropriate their meaning.

From the standpoint of reader-response criticism, it is significant that John uses several techniques for encouraging the reader to identify, and respond to, characteristic features of his narrative world. He presents the paradox, for example, that the Samaritan woman -- a "foreigner" and a non-believer -- unexpectedly becomes a model for growth in Christian discipleship. In a similar way John presents the paradox that "relationship" and "concept" reinforce and enrich each other, although they might seem to conflict with each other as structural elements of Christian life. John also presents the woman's response to Jesus as a model for the response that Christian believers generally can make, as they perceive the initiative that Jesus takes, learn from him, and then testify to him. This response becomes, in turn, a response that the reader is invited to make as a way of actualizing the text. John suggests, finally, that his narrative world has an important similarity to the empirical world of the reader. The narrative world depicts Jesus coming to the woman in the concrete circumstances of her daily life. As real as it is, the narrative world is not an abstraction that has no point of contact with the empirical world. In actualizing the text, the reader recognizes the critical importance of this similarity between the narrative world and the world of everyday human life.

D. Testimony to Jesus

Readers of the Fourth Gospel sometimes wonder why Jesus seems so often to make claims for himself, using the first-person pronoun "I." In 8:12, for instance, Jesus declares, "I am the light of the world. Whoever follows me will never walk in darkness but will have the light of life." It is a very difficult historical question whether John believed that statements of this kind actually represented Jesus' own words, or whether he was intentionally employing this kind of declaration as a vehicle for expressing his own faith through the narrative world of his text. John does recognize, however, that people may react in different ways to Jesus' "I am" statements. Thus in the present passage he indicates that the Pharisees replied to Jesus, "You are testifying on your own behalf; your testimony is not valid" (8:13).

In broad terms, the question of testimony to Jesus becomes the question of authenticating the message of Christian faith, and Jesus' self-testimony represents the self-authenticating quality of Christian revelation. In this sense, John recognizes that Jesus can legitimately engage in self-testimony (8:14). He can testify on his own behalf because there are no other criteria, according to conventional human standards, by which he can be judged (8:15). In a similar way, John suggests, the message of Christian faith may be regarded as self-authenticating because there are no other philosophical or religious criteria in terms of which it could be substantiated. If God made himself known through Christ more fully than in any other way, then other forms of divine revelation can not be used as standards for authenticating the revelation through Christ, regardless of the validity or meaning that they may have in themselves.

Having asserted the intrinsic validity of Jesus' self-testimony, John enlarges the scope of the issue by exploring the significance of relationships as the context in which Jesus can testify on his own behalf. This is also the context, in the final analysis, in which believers can affirm that Jesus is truly the light of the world (8:12). The relationship of Jesus to the Father, John believes, underlies the relationship that Jesus and the Father have to believers, and this relationship in turn helps to determine the structure and content of Christian faith.

It is John's perception that Jesus' relationship to the Father enables him to engage in legitimate testimony to himself, and this testimony in turn enables believers to have "the light of life" (8:12). Jesus testifies on his own behalf, and the Father also testifies on his behalf (8:18). Because two witnesses testify, the testimony is valid (8:17). It should be acceptable, therefore, to those who view the issue according to the requirements of the Jewish law of evidence (cf. Deut. 9:15). In calling attention to this point,

John is not simply meeting the objections of the Pharisees (8:13). He is also indicating that Jesus' self-testimony, as valid as it is, must be seen in the context of his relationship to the Father.

The relationship of the Father to the Son supports the Son and enables him to proclaim that he is "the light of the world" (8:12). Because they hear Jesus' testimony, people have the opportunity to follow Jesus and receive "the light of life" (8:12). To know Jesus, furthermore, is to know the Father also (8:19). In this way, John indicates, the relationship between the Father and the Son underlies and makes possible the relationship that the Father and the Son have to believers. This relationship, in turn, is the essential setting in which Jesus can declare, and believers can affirm, that he is truly the light of the world.

Reader-response criticism in itself is not concerned with the question whether Jesus actually said, "I am the light of the world" (8:12). Nor can it be concerned with the question whether John himself believed that Jesus made this statement. Although these questions are important in historical-critical study, reader-response criticism notes only that John is depicting a narrative world in which Jesus says, "I am the light of the world." In this way John presents a narrative world that the reader will perceive as very different from the everyday world, in which people do not make this kind of claim. It is part of John's technique to impress this difference on the reader. John then proceeds to place Jesus' claim within a broader context, indicating that it expresses the self-authenticating quality of Christian revelation, reflects the relationship between the Son and the Father, and even satisfies the expectations of Jewish law. In these ways John encourages the reader to perceive the paradox that Jesus' statement, which at first establishes a sense of distance between the narrative world and the empirical world, nevertheless has broad ramifications that closely affect the reality of everyday life.

E. The Self-Predication "I Am"

In 8:21-30, John continues to think in terms of the relation between the Father and the Son as the context in which Jesus discusses both his own mission and the nature of Christian faith. In the preceding section (8:11-20), John delineated this relationship by referring to the Father as the one who "sent" Jesus (8:16, 18). Now, in the present passage (8:21-30), he continues to speak of the Father in this way. The Father who "sent" Jesus is true, and Jesus brings words of revelation from him (8:26). In a similar way, the Father who "sent" Jesus remains with him, continuing to support him with his presence (8:29). By repeating the idea of sending, John establishes a verbal link between the preceding passage and the present one. At the same time he indicates that he is continuing to think in terms of the relationship between the Father and the Son as the context in which the content of the passage is meaningful.

In this setting John introduces two new themes: the imminent death of Jesus, and the need for faith in him on the part of those who would receive the life that he offers. Jesus refers to his death by declaring that he is "going away" (8:21) and that he will be "lifted up" (8:28, probably a complex reference to crucifixion, resurrection, and ascension, viewed as aspects of one continuous upward movement in which the Son returns to the Father). Jesus' assertion that he is "not of this world" (8:23) suggests that he regards his death as a return to his home in heaven, rather than an indication of the failure of his work on earth.

From the standpoint of relation analysis, it is especially significant, when Jesus alludes to his own death, that he speaks of God as the father who sent him and continues to be with him (8:29). This is the first time in his gospel that John connects the idea of sending (expressed by the synonyms *apostellō* and *pempō*) with the idea of God's continual presence with Jesus (other possible examples are in 10:35-38 and 17:21, 23). At the time of Jesus' death, John wishes to emphasize, the Father who sent the Son into the world does not leave him alone (*monon*, 8:29) but continues to sustain him with his presence. The relationship between the Father and the Son provides the context in which John can introduce the startling paradox that the one who sends remains present with the one who is sent.

The relationship between the Father and the Son is also intrinsic to the discussion of faith or belief that John presents in this same passage. Jesus offers "the light of life" to his followers (8:12). People, Jesus continues, can receive this life only if they believe that "I am he" (8:24). Jesus' words are literally "I am," *egō eimi*, which represent the Septuagint translation of Yahweh's own self-predication, "I am He," in Second Isaiah. Those who believe in Jesus must be able to perceive and affirm that he is so closely related to God the Father that he can use the same solemn formula of divine self-predication that God himself used in the Old Testament.[19]

The same expression, "I am," recurs in this absolute sense in 8:28: "When you have lifted up the Son of Man, then you will realize that I am he [literally, I am], and that I do nothing on my own, but I speak these things as the Father instructed me." Here the expression "I am" still has its absolute sense, as a reflection of Yahweh's solemn self-predication in Second Isaiah. At the same time, through a double meaning, it can also be supplied with a predicate to mean "I am the Son of Man." Jesus' death, resurrection, and ascension will be the complex event in which believers will be able to perceive the meaning of his role as Son of man and also understand the significance of his declaration, "I am." To believe in Jesus, John implies, is always to see him as the Son who stands in continuing relationship to the Father. Thus in 8:28 it is significant that even when Jesus uses the solemn expression "I am," he emphasizes that he does not act independently but seeks to bring revelation from the Father: "....I do nothing on my own, but I speak these things as the Father instructed me."

John continues to explore the meaning of the relation between Father and Son when he uses the absolute "I am" again in 8:58. Here Jesus declares to the Jews, "Very truly, I tell you, before Abraham was, I am." The Jews, apparently perceiving the meaning of Jesus' divine self-predication, react by taking up stones to throw at him (8:59). A very similar sequence occurs shortly afterward, when Jesus declares, "The Father and I are one" (10:30), and the Jews again react by taking up stones to throw at him (10:31). By indicating that the reaction of the Jews is the same in each case, John suggests that the two statements are virtually equivalent in meaning -- i.e., the declaration "I am" could be paraphrased as "The Father and I are one." Both statements express the divine nature of Jesus and the closeness of his relationship to the Father.

At the same time, John also wants to emphasize that Jesus' statement "I am" in 8:58 is not merely a form of self-assertion. Before he makes this statement, Jesus has pointed out that he honors the Father (8:49), he does not seek his own glory (8:50), he knows the Father and he keeps his word (8:55). John also indicates that the Father, for his part, glorifies the Son (8:50, 54). Each party, that is, voluntarily contributes to the dynamic of a continuing relationship and voluntarily chooses to function within it. It is within this context, John suggests, that Christian believers should understand Jesus' solemn declaration, "I am."

The other occurrences of the self-predication "I am" have reference to the betrayal of Jesus and thus to his imminent death. At the Last Supper, Jesus predicts his betrayal but then explains to the disciples, "I tell you this now, before it occurs, so that when it does occur, you may believe that I am he [I am]" (13:19). Later, when the soldiers and police come to arrest him in the garden, Jesus identifies himself to them with the words "I am he [I am]" (18:5, 6, 8). In an everyday sense, the expression here can mean that Jesus is the person whom they are seeking (cf. 9:9). At the same time, "I am he" is literally "I am," and John is also using it in this sense as the solemn divine self-predication. To emphasize this absolute sense he writes that the soldiers and police, on hearing the words, stepped back and fell to the ground in an attitude of worship (18:6).

John is the only gospel writer to mention Roman soldiers at this point, and the question may be raised whether the soldiers or the police would actually fall to the ground to worship someone whom they were arresting. John wishes to emphasize, however, that an attitude of worship is the appropriate response for anyone to make to the solemn divine self-predication that Jesus utters. John may also be thinking of this incident as a complement to the earlier inquiry of "some Greeks" who wished to see Jesus (12:20 ff.). As the interest of the Greeks established the point that Jesus' ministry was universal in scope, so now the worship of Jesus by the Roman soldiers becomes a way for John to affirm that the universal scope of Jesus' mission is already being realized.

In terms of relation analysis, it is important to recognize that the relational context which John has established for the "I am" sayings in

Chapter 8 also carries over to those in Chapters 13 and 18. In Chapter 8, Jesus makes this declaration within the context of his relationship to the Father, whom he honors and who, in turn, glorifies him. In Chapters 13 and 18, when Jesus uses the self-predication "I am" with reference to his betrayal and death, he is still speaking within the context of his relation to the Father. He is still acting to honor the Father, and he knows that the Father is still seeking to glorify him, even in those events which might seem to represent complete failure and defeat. In this respect John uses the absolute "I am" in a way that is parallel to his use of the verb "glorify" (*doxazō*) to indicate that Jesus is glorified through the complex event of death, resurrection, and ascension to the Father (e.g., 7:39; 12:16, 23; 13:31-32; 17:1, 5).

John treats Jesus' self-predication "I am" in the same way as he treats phrases of self-testimony, such as "I am the light of the world." In both instances he knows that the reader will be surprised at the claims that Jesus makes within the narrative world of the gospel, and in both cases he knows that the reader will sense the difference between the narrative world and the everyday world. In both cases, however, John wants to help the reader actualize the text by finding a way from the one world to the other. In the case of the "I am" statements, John does this by emphasizing that Jesus is not speaking as a solitary religious figure, but as the Son who has been sent by the Father into the world. He does this also by showing that Jesus speaks these words as the one who involves himself in the life of the world, even to the point of giving his life on behalf of others. John indicates, finally, that the appropriate response to Jesus' statement "I am" is an attitude of reverential worship on the part of people in the world. In all these ways, John provides cues that guide the reader in overcoming the difference between the narrative world and the empirical world.

F. Jesus as Resurrection and Life

In Chapter 11, John gives a summary of his understanding of eternal life when he depicts Jesus as saying, "I am the resurrection and the life. Those who believe in me, even though they die, will live, and everyone who lives and believes in me will never die" (11:25-26). Earlier in his gospel John indicated that eternal life is a new quality of life, already available to those who believe in Jesus. Several times John speaks of eternal life in the present tense, or even the perfect tense -- the believer "has" eternal life (3:36; 5:24; 6:47; cf. 6:54; 10:28) and "has passed" from death to life (5:24). Although John defines eternal life only once in his gospel, it is significant that he defines it in terms of relationship -- eternal life is knowing, or standing in relationship to, the only true God and Jesus Christ whom God sent (17:3).

John uses the incident of the raising of Lazarus in Chapter 11 to contrast his understanding of eternal life with the Jewish belief in a future resurrection at the "last day." Martha reflects this belief in talking to Jesus after her brother Lazarus has died (11:24). Jesus qualifies her belief in a future resurrection by transferring it to the present. Here and now, Jesus is the resurrection and the life (11:25a), Jesus offers eternal life to believers (11:25b-26a), and Jesus raises Lazarus as a sign of the present reality of eternal life (11:43-44). Even though some traces of the futurist type of expectation may remain in his gospel (5:28-29; 6:39-40), John thinks of eternal life essentially as a new relationship with God and Christ, a new quality of life that already begins in the present time for those who believe.

Near the very beginning of his gospel John has already suggested the main directions that he will pursue in developing his understanding of eternal life. In the Word of God was "life" (zōe), and then this life was "the light of all people" (1:4). John understands this life as eternal life, whether or not he uses the adjective "eternal" (aiōnios) in any particular instance. John wishes to emphasize, first, that eternal life is not a general religious idea, but a concept specifically connected with the Word of God which became incarnate in Jesus of Nazareth. John also wishes to emphasize that eternal life is communicated through the relationship of the Word to people, as the historical ministry of Jesus made this "life" or "light" available to people in the world. In the remainder of his gospel John will develop these two important aspects of his understanding of eternal life.

John makes it clear, for example, that people do not receive "life" simply by "believing" in general; they receive it specifically by believing in Jesus as the source of life. Several times, it is true, John speaks of believing, without an object, in connection with the reception of life (3:15; 6:47; 20:31).

But in each case the context makes it clear that John is thinking of Jesus as the source of life: the person who believes has life in him (3:15) or in his name (20:31) or on the basis of his role as the bread of life (6:47-48). More directly, John writes several times that the person who believes in Jesus has eternal life (3:16, 36; 6:40). This wording represents more accurately the link that John established in the Prologue (1:4) between the Word and life.

In the same vein, John uses a variety of expressions and figures of speech to express his view that eternal life is given through Jesus. John writes, for example, that Jesus gives water which wells up to eternal life (4:14) and food which endures to eternal life (6:27). Sometimes John mentions "believing" in the context of these statements, calling attention in this way to the importance of the response that people make to Jesus (6:27, 35, 48, 63, 68; 11:25). At other times, without specifically mentioning the act of believing, John simply depicts Jesus as the source of eternal life (4:14; 5:40; 6:51, 54; 8:12; 10:10, 28; 14:6; 17:2). It would be erroneous to assume here, of course, that John is denying the importance of the human response of faith; he is primarily concerned in these passages to present Jesus as the source of eternal life.

John's characteristic view of eternal life is that it is given through Jesus, as Jesus relates to people through his ministry and as people respond by believing in him. In consonance with this view, John thinks of eternal life as an indirect gift, rather than a direct gift, from God the Father. As the Father has life in himself, so he has granted to the Son to have life in himself (5:26). Similarly, the Father gives bread from heaven, and this bread gives life to the world (6:32-33). John speaks only once of "believing" God the Father in connection with the gift of life, and here he also describes God as the one who sent Jesus (5:24; cf. 12:50). In all these instances, from the standpoint of relation analysis, it is significant that the relation of the Father to the Son provides the background for the relation of the Son to people; people, in turn, receive eternal life directly from the Son and, through him, indirectly from the Father.

Sometimes John also uses the verb "live" ($za\bar{o}$) to refer to eternal life. In these instances he uses it in the same ways as he uses the noun "life." Those who believe in Jesus, for example, will live (11:25), and those who hear the voice of the Son of God will live (5:25). Jesus gives living water (4:10; 7:38), and he is himself the living bread (6:51, 58). Because Jesus lives, the disciples will live also (14:19). As the living Father sent Jesus, and Jesus lives because of the Father, so Jesus becomes the source of life for the disciples (6:57). In passages such as these, as in his use of the noun "life," John is thinking in terms of relationships: the relation between the Father and the Son provides the context for the relation between the Son and believers, so that believers receive the gift of life directly from the Son and indirectly from the Father.

The method of relation analysis can help in this way to identify the network of relationships that John weaves into the texture of his thought when he develops his understanding of eternal life. At this point, however, the question arises why John does not simply say that those who believe in God the Father receive eternal life directly from him. Are there any reasons why John presents eternal life as a gift received directly from Jesus, and only indirectly from the Father?

It is possible that John wishes to emphasize in this way the close correspondence of will and action between the Son and the Father, or the obedience that the Son gives to the Father, or the role of the Son in revealing the Father, or the voluntary self-sacrifice of the Son in giving his life that believers may live. John may well have had reasons like these in mind when he focused on the role of Jesus in giving eternal life to those who believe. The fact that the Father is the indirect source of life, John suggests, does not make him any less the ultimate source of life, since Jesus always acts in harmony with the will of the Father. At the same time, John can focus on the role of Jesus as a way of differentiating Christianity from other religions. Christianity is not an example of religion in general, speaking in a general way about the possibility of eternal life; it focuses specifically on Jesus, the Son of God, as the one who made God's gift of eternal life a present reality for believers.

Relation analysis suggests still another reason why John speaks of eternal life as a gift received directly from the Son and indirectly from the Father. When John defines eternal life, he does so in terms of relationships: eternal life is to "know" God and Christ -- i.e., not simply to have an intellectual understanding of them, but actually to be in a living relationship with them (17:3). Through the incarnation, the Son becomes concretely present to people in the midst of their historical existence. He is there with them, so that they can believe in him and enter into relation to him as his followers. People, that is, can enter into a relationship with the Son in a direct way. Because the Son reveals the Father (1:18), people can come to know the Father through the Son. Thus their relation to the Son is direct and their relation to the Father is indirect, as it is mediated through the revelation by the Son. In an analogous way, John suggests, people receive eternal life directly from the Son and indirectly from God the Father.

John may well expect that the typical reader will think, in a very general way, of believing in God and thus receiving eternal life. Perhaps for this reason John is so careful to delineate a narrative world in which people, by believing in the Son, receive eternal life directly from the Son and indirectly from the Father. Just as the reception of eternal life reflects the relationship between the Father and the Son, so eternal life itself, John indicates, consists of living relationship with the Father and the Son. In these ways John seeks to make the reader aware of salient features of this complex belief that the reader is asked to affirm. To help the reader in making this affirmation, John also gives a number of examples within the text of people who respond to Jesus by believing in him and thus receiving eternal life.

G. God's Love for Believers

The methodology of relation analysis is concerned with the meaning of love as a particular subject expresses love toward an object, and also with the parallels or similarities between situations involving different subjects or objects. The section of the preceding chapter entitled "The Father's Love for the Son" analyzed the relationship of love existing within the Godhead itself, usually with the Father as subject and the Son as object. The present section will investigate the structure of love between God and people, usually with God as the subject and believers as the object. Relation analysis can look at each situation separately and then take the further step of comparing the two situations. This kind of comparison can identify patterns of continuity in

John's thought as he turns from one relationship to another, and it also suggests how the structure of one relationship can underlie that of another.

The analysis of the love that the Father showed to the Son suggested that this love was a continuing, unchanging love that has always characterized the attitude of the Father toward the Son. This love also involved a reciprocal relationship, since the Son loves the Father. The Father's love for the Son was a dynamic love, expressing itself in specific actions on behalf of its object. It reflected wholehearted trust in the Son, bestowing power on its object. It was closely associated with the gift of eternal life, which had its ultimate source in the Father and its proximate source in the Son. The Father's love was unconditional, having no cause other than itself. Paradoxically, it was also contingent, since it responded to the action of the Son in voluntarily laying down his life for others. It is indicative of the texture of John's thought that the present analysis of the love between God and believers will show parallels to a number of these characteristics of the love between the Father and the Son.

John's first use of the word "love," as a verb or a noun, occurs in the verse that is perhaps the best known of his gospel: "For God so loved the world that he gave his only Son, so that everyone who believes in him may not perish but may have eternal life" (3:16). At this point the term "world" seems to include all people, seen here, at least potentially, as capable of making the response of faith. The verse indicates that God's love itself is directed to all and is offered to all. God's love does not simply involve attitude or intention, but it expresses itself in concrete action: "God so loved... that he gave..." In a similar way, it is directed toward a specific goal: "so that everyone who believes in him... may have eternal life." If the beginning of the verse refers to all people, as potential believers, then the close of the verse refers more explicitly to those who actually make the response of faith. When John speaks of God's love, he thinks in terms of relationships which he delineates as clearly as possible. These relationships involve God, his only Son, the world, and everyone who believes.

This central verse shows that God's love for the world, like the Father's love for the Son, is an active, dynamic love that seeks to benefit its object: "God so loved... that he gave..." (3:16; cf. 3:35). John seems to be thinking in terms of a love that by its very nature seeks to find expression in an action that promotes the best interests and enhances the well-being of its object. It is perhaps a moot question what John would think of other types of love, which seek, for example, to contemplate the object, admire the beauty or virtue of the object, rejoice in sharing friendship with the object, or receive something from the object. John does not speak of these other types of love, apparently because he is thinking of love so exclusively as an active love that seeks to benefit its object. In the structure of John's thought there may well be a connection between the Father's love for the Son and God's love for the world -- as the Father loves the Son and has given all things to him (3:35), so God loved the world and gave his Son to the world (3:16). From its eternal source within the Godhead, love, for John, involves giving to its object.

The parallelism between 3:35 and 3:16 also calls attention to the costly nature of God's love. The Father loves the Son and has given all things to the Son (3:35), presumably because the Father, in his love, perceived that it would be in the best interests of the Son to have this power over all things. So the Father limited himself, voluntarily giving power to the Son and allowing him, for example, to grant eternal life to those who believe in him (cf. 3:36). In this respect the Father's love for the Son was costly to himself. In a similar Way God's love for the world was costly, for it meant loving the world to the point of being willing to give his Son to the world (3:16). The fact that the Son voluntarily laid down his life for the world did not mean that God's initial act of giving his Son was less costly. The parallelism between 3:35 and 3:16 suggests that the costliness of love, as John understands it, has its source in the relationships within the Godhead itself.

As the Father's love for the Son has no cause other than itself, so, John believes, God's love for the world has no cause other than itself. John does not say that God loved the world because of any quality inhering in the world itself, or because people first earned his love, or for any other reason. Indeed, John has already called attention to the tragic fact that the world has, at least in many instances, rejected "the true light" (1:9-10), and he repeats in the present context that "people loved darkness rather than light because their deeds were evil" (3:19). John must believe that God loved the world because he is a loving God: God loved because he loved. The wonder of God's love, John suggests, must derive from the very fact of its tautology.

If John sees no need to give a cause for God's love for the world, he does give a proximate result, a purpose, and an eventual or ultimate result. God's love has a proximate result, expressed by *hōste*, that has already occurred: "God so loved... that he gave..." (3:16). John would be thinking at this point of the incarnation and the earthly ministry of the Son, including his death on behalf of the world. In a similar way John writes that God's love has a purpose, expressed by *hina*, that is still being realized: "so that everyone who believes in him... may have eternal life" (3:16). As he establishes a close connection between loving, giving, and eternal life in 3:35, so John makes this same connection in 3:16. The connection, that is, is present in relation to the Father's love for the Son, and it continues now in relation to God's love for the world. John probably has the same connection in mind in the following verse, in which he states that God sent the Son into the World "in order that the world might be saved through him" (3:17). Receiving eternal life and receiving salvation, for John, seem to be equivalent concepts. God's purpose in offering eternal life leads, in turn, to a general or eventual result -- those who believe in the Son are not condemned, but those who do not believe are condemned already (3:18).

In 3:16, John has used the term "world" (*kosmos*) for the first time since the opening chapter of his gospel. He indicated there that "the true light... was coming into the world" (1:9). He also described the tragedy of the world's reaction to the light: "He was in the world, and the world came into being through him; yet the world did not know him" (1:10; cf. 3:19). In spite of this negative response on the part of the world, John could also describe Jesus as "the Lamb of God who takes away the sin of the world" (1:29).

John presupposes these earlier statements about the "world" when he uses the term again in 3:16. The new thought that he introduces at this point is that God loved the world. In this way John suggests that his earlier statements about the world, as central as they are, must be seen in the light of God's love for the world and the relationship that this love establishes between God and the people in the world. When Christians believe in God as a loving God, they are believing in the God who has chosen to establish this relationship with the people of the world. In principle, at least, God's love for the "world" not only includes actual believers, as important as their role is, but it also extends to all persons everywhere, whom John would think of as potential believers.

A significant parallel between the Father's love for the Son and God's love for people is that both types of love are unconditional and then, within this context, also contingent. The Father's love for the Son has, in principle, no cause other than itself, yet the Father can also love the Son because the Son voluntarily lays down his life for others (10:17-18). The unconditional love of the Father for the Son establishes the relationship within which the Father can also respond positively to the deeds of the Son. The Father, as the active God who works in history, can respond in this way to events occurring within the arena of history. Presumably, in John's view, the Father would love the Son no less even if the Son did not lay down his life for others. Without entering into calculations concerning the quantity or the quality of the Father's love, John wishes to indicate only that the Father does care about the actions of the Son and does respond in love to the work of the Son.

In a very similar way, John thinks of God's love for the world as uncaused and unconditional, and yet responsive. The world has not done anything to earn God's love; indeed, people have often rejected the "true light" and have loved darkness rather than light (1:9-10; 3:19). In this sense, God can love the world only because he is a loving God. Yet John also indicates that God loves believers because of their attitudes and their deeds -- God loves them because they have believed that Jesus came from God (16:27), because they love Jesus (14:21, 23; 16:27), and because they keep his commandments (14:15, 21, 23-24). God's love for believers, that is, can be a response to their own faith, love, and deeds. As in the case of the Father's love for the Son, God's love for believers reflects the fact that God is an active God who takes account of, and responds positively to, the events that occur in history. God's unconditional love for the world establishes the relationship within which he can respond in love to the faith, love, and action of believers.

It is indeed a paradox that the Father's love for the Son, and God's love for people, can be unconditional and also contingent. It is very possible, in view of the many parallels that John draws between them, that John would regard the Father's relationship to the Son as the ultimate source and model for God's relationship to the world. John seems content, however, to accept the paradox that love can be both unconditional and contingent. Each aspect expresses an important truth -- love is unconditional because God is a loving God, and it is contingent because God cares about the actions of the other party within a relationship. Precisely because God does love the other party, he wants the relationship to be real for that party, and so he cares about the responses that the other party makes. John seems to recognize why God's love is unconditional and why it is contingent. He prefers to accept the paradox that it is both, rather than lose sight of the truth that either aspect expresses.

If God loves believers, and if God cares about the responses that believers make within his relationship to them, then it should follow that John would emphasize the need for believers to love God. The writer of the First Letter of John does not hesitate to speak of the love that people have for God -- e.g., "those who love God must love their brothers and sisters also" (I John 4:21; cf. I John 2:5, 15; 3:17; 4:20; 5:1-3). It is necessary to leave this letter out of consideration, however, because its author may not have actually been the same person as the John who wrote the gospel. The data indicate that in the Gospel of John itself there are very few references to situations in which people show love for God.

A passage in which Jesus is speaking to some Jews is characteristic of the viewpoint that John reflects: "Jesus said to them, 'If God were your Father, you would love me, for I came from God and now I am here...'" (8:42). In positive terms, John is indicating that to have God as one's Father means to have love for Jesus. It would seem completely reasonable at this point for John to speak of loving God as well, but he does not do so. Indeed, he very rarely alludes to the love that people have for God. He does refer at one point to the importance of loving "the glory that comes from God" (12:43), but here he is distinguishing different kinds of glory rather than speaking directly of loving God (cf. 5:44). John does refer in 5:42 to "the love of God," which the Jews, in this instance, do not have. Presumably the genitive here is objective, so that the phrase refers to the love that people show to God. But it is only in this indirect way that John calls attention to the importance of loving God. When John is speaking directly of the spiritual life of Christian believers, it is surprising that he never actually mentions that they are to love God.

Presumably John would not object in itself to the idea that believers should love God as part of their Christian life. The reason why he scarcely mentions this idea seems to be that he is thinking in terms of complex relationships. He reflects this outlook when he is thinking of other topics, such as revelation, eternal life, and religious faith. John indicates, for example, that God does not reveal himself directly to people (1:18). The Father is related to the Son, and the Son makes the Father known to believers; conversely, believers enter into relationship with the Son, and then through him with the Father. John consistently thinks of Jesus as the middle term, as it were, between God and people.

In a similar way, when John is speaking of eternal life, he presents Jesus as the immediate source of life, even though the Father remains the ultimate source. When John is speaking of religious faith, using the expression "believe in" (*pisteuō eis*), he almost always speaks of believing in Jesus. Only on two occasions does John speak of believing directly in God, and in both instances he also speaks of believing in Jesus: "Whoever believes in me believes not in me but in him who sent me" (12:44), and "Believe in God, believe also in me" (14:1).[20] Even in these instances, when he speaks of believing directly in God, John is thinking in terms of believing in Jesus within the context of the relationship between God and Jesus.

John evidently thinks of loving God in the same way that he thinks of receiving revelation, obtaining eternal life, and believing in God. In all these instances he is reluctant to speak in terms of a direct relationship between the believer and God, as if this relationship could exist in any significant way apart from the work of Jesus. John is so convinced of the critical significance of Jesus in revealing God and mediating the gifts of salvation that he almost always thinks in terms of a direct relationship between believers and Jesus, and an indirect relationship between believers and God. The first relationship makes possible the second, and the second is more real, rather than less, because of the first. Precisely because of the work of Jesus, the end result is that believers can truly love God, receive eternal life from God, and believe in God. As a reflection of the relational structure of his thought, however, John usually speaks instead of loving Jesus, receiving eternal life from Jesus, and believing in Jesus.

Just as he speaks of God's love for the world or for believers, John also speaks of Jesus' love for believers. Thus he writes that Jesus loves Lazarus (11:3, 36), Martha, Mary, and Lazarus (11:5), "his own" (13:1), and an unnamed disciple (13:23; 19:26; 20:2; 21:7, 20). Like God's own love for the world, Jesus' love for believers is an active love that promotes the well-being of its object. Thus Jesus raises Lazarus, reassures Martha and Mary, and even dies on behalf of "his own." Like the Father's love for the Son, and God's love for the world, Jesus' love for believers has no cause other than itself. In this respect Jesus continues to illustrate the motif of unconditional love. Since it is Jesus' love that affects people most directly, it is significant that John thinks of this love as offered freely, without cause or condition.

At the same time, John introduces again the paradox that love can be unconditional and also contingent. The Father's love for the Son had both characteristics, and God's love for the world had the same characteristics. Now, John indicates, Jesus' love for his followers can be understood as unconditional and also as contingent. Jesus offers his love freely, but he also loves those who love him (14:21) and keep his commandments (14:21; 15:10; cf. 15:14). Jesus' unconditional love is needed to initiate the relationship that he seeks with believers. But Jesus also seeks a relationship that will be real for the believers themselves, giving them the opportunity to participate in it and make an active contribution to it. For this reason Jesus responds positively to the attitude of love and the works of obedience that believers exhibit. Because he cares about his followers, Jesus cares how they respond within the relationship that he has made possible.

Jesus' words to his disciples in the Farewell Discourses illustrate how the concept of "abiding" joins together the unconditional and the contingent aspects of his love: "As the Father has loved me, so I have loved you; abide in my love. If you keep my commandments, you will abide in my love, just as I have kept my Father's commandments and abide in his love" (15:9-10). As the Father loved the Son with an unconditional love, so Jesus has loved the disciples unconditionally and thus has made possible a new relationship with them. Now Jesus asks the disciples to abide in "my love," an expression in which "my" is equivalent to a subjective genitive -- the disciples, that is, are to remain in the love that Jesus has shown to them. They can do this if they keep the commandments that Jesus has given them. Jesus, in this respect, loves those who keep his commandments. Jesus' unconditional love for his followers establishes a new relationship, and his contingent love recognizes their efforts to "abide" within this relationship by loving him and keeping his commandments.

John does not seem to mean that Jesus' love is unconditional at first and then becomes contingent as he directs it to those who have responded by loving him and keeping his commandments. John probably believes that Jesus' unconditional love always remains in effect, as a controlling factor, instead of being changed into a different type of love. But John also wants to indicate that the relationship between Jesus and his disciples is a living, dynamic relationship, rather than simply a state. Because Jesus wants his disciples to appreciate this relationship and live meaningfully within it, he responds in love to the attempts that they make to show love and obedience of their own. Jesus' unconditional love, therefore, is not transformed into contingent love, but it provides the context in which his contingent love can assume its appropriate function.

In accordance with this view that Jesus' love for believers is both unconditional and contingent, John puts considerable emphasis on the expectation that believers will respond to Jesus with love and obedience of their own. Keeping Jesus' commandments becomes a way of remaining or "abiding" in the love that Jesus has shown them (15:9-10). Loving Jesus is a way of acknowledging that God is their Father (cf. 8:42), and it becomes in turn one reason why the Father loves believers (16:27). Loving Jesus, as Jesus explains to Peter in the closing chapter of the gospel, is a necessary condition for undertaking the work of ministry to others (21:15-17). In all of these ways John indicates how seriously he regards the importance of the response that believers make to the love that Jesus has shown to them.

John emphasizes most clearly the importance of this response in establishing the basic connection between loving Jesus and keeping his commandments (14:15, 21, 23-24). This connection in turn has significant consequences for the structure of Christian life. Those who love Jesus and give obedience to his commandments will be loved by the Father (14:21, 23) and by Jesus (14:21); Jesus will reveal himself to them (14:21), and Jesus and the Father will come to them and make their home (*monē*, dwelling place) with them (14:23). Although Jesus and the Father both offer an unconditional love as the basis for establishing the initial relationship with believers, they also respond in these important ways to the love and obedience that believers themselves show within this relationship. If John does not emphasize the love that believers show directly to the Father, he does underline the need for their love and obedience to Jesus himself.

Although John does not use the word "covenant" (*diathēkē*), the close connection that he establishes between the believers' love for Jesus and their obedience to his commandments echoes the understanding of the covenant relationship presented in the Old Testament, especially in the book of Deuteronomy. D. R. Hillers has pointed out that "love" in Deuteronomy is not simply an emotion but a response to God that can be commanded: "You shall love the Lord your God with all your heart, and with all your soul, and with all your might" (Deut. 6:5). Love, furthermore, is intrinsically connected with obedience to God: "You shall love the Lord your God, therefore, and keep his charge, his decrees, his ordinances, and his commandments always" (Deut. 11:1). With reference to the work of W. L. Moran, Hillers points out further that this understanding of the love of God has its secular source in the language of diplomacy and treaties, beginning with the Amarna letters. To love, in this sense, means to recognize someone else as a treaty partner (an equal partner, a vassal, or a suzerain, depending on the type of treaty), and for a vassal it means to show loyalty and obedience to a suzerain. Hillers points out that "love of God" as an ancient covenant idea appears more clearly in Deuteronomy than in any other Old Testament writing.[21] It is significant that John, without using the term "covenant," preserves this aspect of covenant thought when he links the love that believers are to show to Jesus with their obligation to obey his commandments.

John uses three narrative devices -- parallelism, paradox, and omission -- as strategies for alerting the reader to the distinctive characteristics of God's love for believers. John shows, for example, that this love has a number of parallels to the Father's love for the Son: it is active and dynamic, it is costly, it has no cause other than itself, it seeks an appropriate response. In a similar way, John brings out a number of parallels between God's love for believers and Jesus' own love for believers. John uses paradox when he depicts God's love for believers, and Jesus' love for believers, as unconditional and at the same time contingent, just as he depicted the Father's love for the Son in the same terms. John also uses omission as a literary technique, since he passes over almost completely the idea that believers should love God, emphasizing instead that they should show love and obedience to Jesus. Through these strategies John is depicting a narrative world that the reader might not expect. If the reader is to affirm this world, John is, in effect, encouraging the reader to become aware of the many dimensions of God's love for Christian believers and the correlations among the several forms of relationship in which love occurs.

H. Believing and Doing

A special issue that arises in the study of any biblical book is the question how the author understands the process of entering into relationship with God and receiving the gifts or benefits that are intrinsic to this relationship, such as forgiveness, salvation, or eternal life. The terms that are used to describe this new relationship with God and the benefits that it bestows will vary according to the perspectives and vocabulary of a specific author. The apostle Paul, for example, often speaks in terms of receiving justification or salvation, being justified or saved, or inheriting the kingdom of God. John uses these particular terms very rarely or not at all. He prefers instead to speak of receiving "eternal life" ($z\bar{o}e$ $ai\bar{o}nios$) or, with the same meaning, simply "life" ($z\bar{o}e$). Although Paul uses these expressions as well, John seems to regard them as central terms for expressing his understanding of the nature and consequences of the Christian's relationship to God.

Closely related to the question of describing the new relationship with God is the problem of determining how people may receive it. In theory, they may receive it as a gift, as a reward, or through some combination of gift and reward. If people could not possibly do enough to earn a new relationship with God, then they can approach God only on the basis of their faith, and they can receive their new relationship with him only as a gift. On the other hand, if people could present their own ethical achievements, acts of service, or other "good works" as a sufficient basis for receiving a new relationship with God, then they would receive this status as a reward for their accomplishments. In theory, it is also possible that some synergistic combination of "faith" and "works" would provide the basis for receiving the new relation with God and appropriating the benefits that it bestows.

Paul's solution to this question helps to define the problem as it arises with regard to John. Alluding to Ps. 143:2, Paul stressed that no one can be justified "on the basis of works of law" (*ex ergōn nomou*, Rom. 3:20; Ga. 2:16). People can be justified only by God's "grace" (*chariti*, Rom. 3:20), which they receive "as a gift" (*dōrean*, Rom. 3:20). Expressing the same idea from the point of view of people, Paul argues that they are justified "on the basis of faith" (*ek pisteōs*, Rom. 3:26, 30; 5:1; Gal. 2:16; 3:8, 24) or "by faith" (*pistei*, Rom. 3:28). Paul wished to emphasize that Christians do not earn their new relationship with God, in whole or in part; they can receive it only as a gift, in faith. Christians are, indeed, concerned to do "good works," but they do these as ways of giving expression to their new relationship with God rather than as ways of earning it (cf. Gal. 5:6, 13-14, 25).

John does not use the verb "justify" (*dikaioō*) or the noun "faith" (*pistis*). Rather than speaking of being "justified," John prefers to speak of receiving "life" or "eternal life," as a comprehensive term referring both to the new relationship with God and to the benefits that it confers. Occasionally John uses other expressions, such as being "saved" or becoming "children of God," which seem to be alternate ways of referring to his central concept of receiving "life." Although he avoids the noun "faith," John does use the verb "believe" (*pisteuō*), which derives from the same stem, and in this way he emphasizes the importance of "believing" as an ongoing activity of Christian life.

In a manner that is parallel to Paul's view of faith as the basis for justification, John often speaks of "believing" as the basis for receiving eternal life. Those who believe in Jesus as Son of man, for example, receive eternal life (3:15). Those who believe in Jesus as Son of God are not condemned (3:18) but have eternal life (3:16, 36). Those who hear Jesus' word and believe the one who sent him have eternal life (5:24). All who believe in Jesus as the bread of life receive eternal life (6:33-40; cf. 6:47). Those who believe in Jesus will "live," i.e., never die (11:25-26). In a similar vein, John writes that those who believe in Jesus receive power to become "children of God" (1:12), and those who believe in "the light" become "children of light" (12:36). Indeed, the very purpose of his gospel, John indicates, is that readers may believe, and "through believing... may have life in his name" (20:31).

In these ways John makes it clear that he regards "believing" as the basis for receiving eternal life. Usually he speaks specifically of believing in Jesus, in his role as Son of man, Son of God, or bread of life. Even when he speaks simply of "believing," John indicates by the context that he is thinking of believing in Jesus (cf. 6:47; 7:38). Eternal life, for John, is not a general religious concept but a specific gift that people receive through believing in Jesus. Although it derives ultimately from God the Father, it is a gift that the Father has granted the Son to bestow (5:21, 26).

Along with this principle that "believing" is the basis for receiving eternal life, John, paradoxically, sometimes seems to reflect the view that "doing" good works, or "believing" and "doing" together, are actually necessary as a condition for receiving life. At a number of points, that is, John speaks of doing good deeds, obeying Jesus, keeping his commandments, and loving him in connection with the reception of eternal life. These references to "good works" seem to suggest, at least, that John had not developed a consistent view of the dynamics of Christian life or perhaps that he had a tendency to think in synergistic terms.

A number of passages illustrate the problem that John presents when he speaks of "doing," or "believing" and "doing" together. In Chapter 3, for example, John makes it clear that believing in Jesus is fundamental; those who believe in him are not condemned (3:18). But then John also emphasizes the importance of the deeds that people do. Those who "do what is true" are willing to have their deeds examined "so that it may be clearly seen that their deeds have been done in God" (3:21). By linking the themes of believing and doing in this way, John may be implying that the first must express itself in the second, in such a way that both together constitute the basis for receiving eternal life.

The idea of "following" Jesus also illustrates this problem of correlating the themes of "believing" and "doing." Those who follow Jesus, John writes, will have "the light of life" (8:12). In a similar way, Jesus' sheep hear his voice, follow him, and receive eternal life (10:27-28). In both instances the idea of following Jesus undoubtedly includes having faith in him, but it may also include living in the way that Jesus wishes for his disciples to live. John gives the impression, at least, that he is thinking here of "believing" and "doing" together as establishing the basis for the reception of eternal life.

In a number of other passages also John speaks of human ethical activity in conjunction with the reception of eternal life. In one of the few passages in which he reflects a futuristic eschatology, he writes that "those who have done good" will rise to "the resurrection of life" (5:29). Elsewhere he reassures his readers that whoever keeps the word of Jesus "will never see death" (8:51). John emphasizes that those who love Jesus will keep his word, and then Jesus and the Father will come to them and make their "home" with them (14:20-24). John indicates, finally, that the disciples are "friends" of Jesus if they do what he commands them (15:14). In all these instances John seems to be thinking in terms of a sequence in which some form of ethical activity leads to a spiritual goal such as acceptance by God or the reception of eternal life.

Much more than Paul, John seems willing to risk using a synergistic terminology in which faith and works, "believing" and "doing," interact with one another and together establish the basis for receiving salvation or eternal life. Perhaps John was writing for readers who were, in many instances, of Jewish background, and he wished to reassure them of the continuing importance of the ethical component in Christian life. Perhaps John, like Matthew, wished to stress the importance of morality in the early church generally, even though he did not record a detailed *didachē* or collection of Jesus' ethical teachings. Perhaps John, writing half a century later than Paul, felt that he could emphasize the need for ethics without raising the problem of legalism, precisely because the issue of faith *versus* works had been decided long ago. Whatever the reason, John clearly stresses the theme of "doing" as well as "believing" in his presentation of Christian discipleship.

The methodology of relation analysis provides some help at this point by suggesting that John's presentation of the themes of "believing" and "doing" may be understood within the broader context of the relationship that he depicts between Jesus and the disciples. John is especially concerned to explain the structure of this relationship in the second half of his gospel, in which he presents the Last Supper and then the Farewell Discourses. This relationship between Jesus and the disciples extends, in turn, to the continuing relation between the risen Lord and his followers of later generations.

Jesus' actions at the Last Supper are especially important in establishing the opportunities that the disciples receive to enter into relationship with him. As Teacher and Lord, Jesus has washed the feet of the disciples, and now he commands them that they should wash one another's feet: "So if I, your Lord and Teacher, have washed your feet, you also ought to wash one another's feet" (13:14). His action on their behalf has made it possible for them to have a new relationship with him, a "share" with him (13:8). Now, in turn, they are to express this relationship by their actions toward one another. Just as Jesus has loved them, they are to love one another (13:34).

In this way John depicts the context in which the motifs of "believing" and "doing" must be understood. Jesus has taken the initiative and performed an action making it possible for the disciples to enter into relation with him. When they believe in him, they perceive him as Teacher and Lord, and they accept his action on their behalf. Their relationship to Jesus becomes real for them through their believing in him. Then they give expression to this relationship through deeds of service to one another. "Believing" becomes the basis on which the disciples receive and appropriate their relation to Jesus, and "doing" refers to the way in which they express this relation in the concrete circumstances of life. Since Jesus himself has taken the initiative to offer the relationship, and the acts of "believing" and "doing" take place within this relationship, the disciples do not earn the relationship through their own efforts. Thus John, in the language of later times, avoids the semi-Pelagianism that seems to be suggested by his emphasis on "doing" as well as "believing."

This analysis of the footwashing at the Last Supper would also apply to Jesus' sacrificial death on the cross, since it is very likely that John thinks of the footwashing as a preenactment of Jesus' death. Just as Jesus assumes the role of servant and washes the disciples' feet, so he will very shortly offer his life on their behalf. The first event becomes a proleptic statement of the meaning of the second. John establishes this connection by alluding to Jesus' death just before (13:1) and just after (13:31-33) his account of the footwashing. In a very similar way he indicates the connection by using the verb "love" (*agapaō*) as a "dramatic aorist" before (13:1) and after (13:34) the footwashing. In both verses the past tense vividly depicts an imminent event as having already occurred. Jesus, John suggests, "has loved" the disciples, not only in washing their feet, but in laying down his life on their behalf. John also suggests the connection between these two events by using the phrase *eis telos* (13:1) with a double meaning: for Jesus to love the disciples "to the end" of his life was to love them "completely." Jesus' death on behalf of the disciples was, at the same time, the perfect expression of his redemptive love for them.

If the footwashing foreshadows the death of Jesus in this way, then again John wishes to indicate that the disciples' relationship with Jesus becomes the context in which their "believing" and "doing" must be understood. The sacrificial death of Jesus establishes the possibility for believers to have a new relationship with him. Believers themselves can not do anything to make this relation possible. Only by accepting Jesus' action on their behalf can they have a "share" with him (13:8). They appropriate this possibility by believing in Jesus as "Lord" and "God," sharing, in effect, in the confession of Thomas, even though they may belong to later generations of followers "who have not seen and yet have come to believe" (20:29). Whether they belong to the original circle of disciples or to later generations of believers, the followers of Jesus are commanded to express their relationship to him by showing love to one another, just as Jesus himself loved them (13:34).

In 15:1-5, John employs the concept of "abiding" as a middle term between the motifs of "believing" and "doing." He depicts Jesus here as the vine, and his disciples as the branches. Only by abiding in Jesus can the disciples bear fruit: "I am the vine," Jesus says, "you are the branches. Those who abide in me and I in them bear much fruit, because apart from me you can do nothing" (15:5). The disciples' relationship to Jesus has been made possible by his redemptive actions on their behalf (13:1-35). John evidently assumes here, as in 20:28, that the disciples appropriate this relation by responding in faith. Then they give expression to the relationship in the works that they do, the "fruit" that they bear. In this way they "prove to be" (not "become") Jesus' disciples (15:8). "Believing" leads to "abiding," and "abiding," as a metaphor for continuing relationship with Jesus, expresses itself in "doing" the good deeds of ethical activity. "Abiding" in Jesus is the necessary condition for "doing" good works (15:4-5), and genuine "abiding," conversely, can have no other result than bearing the fruits of ethical living (15:2).

By focusing on the dynamics of the relationship between Jesus and believers, the method of relation analysis indicates that John, no less than Paul, regards "grace" rather than "works" as the basis on which people may receive new possibilities for fullness of life. Paul typically speaks of faith as the basis for justification, while John usually speaks of believing as the condition for receiving eternal life. John, at the same time, is less careful than Paul in avoiding synergistic language. Yet relation analysis indicates that John focuses on Jesus' redemptive actions as the sole basis for the relationship that the disciples may receive with him. In a similar way, John emphasizes the faith of the disciples, rather than their ethical achievement, as the means by which they appropriate and enter the life-giving relationship with their Lord. John thinks of this relationship, finally, as the context in which, and from which, the disciples engage in ethical activity, loving as they have been loved and bearing fruit as branches abiding in the vine.

John's emphasis on the relationship between Jesus and his followers becomes the primary strategy by which he helps the reader deal with the problem of correlating faith and works, "believing" and "doing." John may be addressing readers who, he thinks, stress the importance of faith; conversely, he may be assuming that his readers will emphasize the need for good works. He may also think that his readers have a tendency to think in terms of a rigid contrast between faith and works, apart from the broader relational context in which they must be understood. By focusing on Jesus' redemptive actions as the basis for the relationship that Jesus offers to believers, John can present this relationship as the context in which "believing" and "doing" have their appropriate roles in Christian life. In this way John provides theologically responsible direction for the reader who wishes to actualize the text of the gospel and enter its narrative world.

CHAPTER III

Believers and Believers: The Community of Faith

A. Children of God

In general, each chapter in this study presupposes the preceding ones. Thus the present chapter, which deals with Christian believers in the community of faith, assumes that believers understand their faith as it has its source in the relationships among Father, Son, and Spirit, and as it receives form and content in the relationship of God to people. In this general sense John has been concerned with the community of faith from the very beginning of his gospel.

In another sense also John begins very early in his gospel to explore the meaning of the community of faith. It is significant that in the Prologue, John uses the language of relationships, not only in speaking of the Word and God, but also in speaking of believers and God. Believers are enlightened by the "true light" (1:9), and they receive him by believing in his name (1:12). In this way they become "children of God" (1:12), entering into a relationship with God that goes beyond any inherited status or natural endowment (1:13). Their new relationship with God significantly defines their existence and essence, just as for the Word itself existence and essence are closely related to the forms of relationship that the Word assumes.

The reference in 1:12 to those who "believed in his name" and "received power to become children of God" must underlie and make possible the use of "we" and "us" in the following verses (1:14, 16). John seems to introduce these first-person pronouns casually, but he must be thinking of Christian believers -- those who have seen the glory of the incarnate Word (1:14) and have received "from his fullness... grace upon grace" (1:16). Believing, John suggests, underlies seeing and receiving, much as, in synoptic tradition, the confession of faith at Caesarea Philippi precedes the perception of the divine glory of Jesus at the transfiguration (e.g., Mk. 8:27-30; 9:2-8). The pronouns "we" and "us," furthermore, imply a community of believers whose members are related to one another on the basis of their relation to the incarnate Word. By believing, seeing, and receiving, they become "we" and "us," members of a community sharing in the gifts of God's grace.

In terms of reader-response criticism, the use of "we" and "us" becomes a technique by which John a) identifies himself, the actual author, with the implied author who is responsible for the specific set of beliefs expressed in the text, and then b) directly addresses the actual reader and invites this reader to identify with the implied reader in the text, accepting the values and beliefs that the implied reader affirms. Through this simple device of using "we" and "us," John indicates the direction that he hopes the real reader will follow throughout the gospel. Otherwise John is usually content to present a text in which an implied author is addressing an implied reader.

In the Prologue, John suggests further that the relationship of believers to one another is mediate, deriving from their relation to the Word. Through believing in the Word they are related, in the first instance, to God, and by sharing in this relationship to God they also become related to one another. As children of God, they become, in effect, fellow believers within the community of faith. By depicting the community of faith in this way, John stresses the primary and continuing significance of the relationship to God that all believers share. Within this context John will turn, in later chapters, to the ways in which believers are related more directly to one another.

B. The Bread of Life: Patterns of Response

It is in Chapter 6 that John specifically turns his attention for the first time to the religious life of the early Christian community. Up to this point he has been focusing primarily on other topics and other types of relationship. Now, in Chapter 6, he relates the feeding of the 5,000, the incident of Jesus' walking on the water, and several ensuing discourses. John treats this material in a way which indicates that he is thinking about the meaning of the celebration of the Lord's Supper in the Christian community. He points out, for example, that the feeding of the 5,000 occurred near the time of Passover, the season of the year when the Last Supper itself took place (6:4). In describing the feeding he speaks of bread and fish (6:11), but then in a subsequent discourse he shifts to the terminology of eating and drinking, as a reflection of the extent to which he is thinking in terms of the bread and the wine at the Lord's supper (6:35, 53-56). Although all four gospels relate the feeding of the 5,000, John alone uses the verb "give thanks" (*eucharisteō*) in describing Jesus' actions (6:11); the Synoptics use this verb in their accounts of the Last Supper (Matt. 26:27; Mk. 14:23; Lk. 22:17, 19), but not in connection with the feeding of the 5,000. In ways such as these, John indicates that he is regarding the feeding of the 5,000 as a type or model for the understanding of the meaning of the Lord's Supper in the early church.

It may seem surprising that John would deal with the Lord's Supper on the first occasion on which he specifically treats the religious life of the early Christian community. In some respects John seems to avoid any emphasis, or at least any overemphasis, on the sacraments. In relating the work of John the Baptist, for example, John omits any mention of the actual baptism of Jesus. In a similar way, he omits any reference to the bread and the wine in his portrayal of the Last Supper in Chapter 13. The baptism of Jesus and the distribution of the bread and the wine at the Last Supper provided the basis in Jesus' own life for the church's observance of the sacraments of baptism and the Lord's Supper. John makes no mention, however, of these events.

One possible reason why John may have passed over these incidents is that he wished to counter a tendency in the early church to overemphasize the efficacy of the sacraments in themselves, as if they operated in a mechanical, *ex opere operato* fashion. According to this interpretation, John would not be opposing the use of the sacraments themselves. He would be objecting only to an overemphasis which regarded them as an automatic means of grace, apart from the faith and attitude of the participants, or apart from their effect in Christian life. Thus in his account of the Last Supper, for example, John depicts Jesus washing the feet of the disciples as a model for the kind of loving service that should characterize the lives of all Christians as a result of their participation in the sacramental life of the church. Without this kind of result, John implies, Christians may fail to perceive the relation of worship to life, and they may understand the sacraments only as a mechanical means of grace.

If this interpretation is correct, it becomes all the more surprising that John deals with the Lord's Supper the first time he turns his attention directly to the life of the early Christian community. It is important to note, however, that John is careful to avoid any overemphasis on the Lord's Supper as a mechanical means of grace. To avoid an excessive concentration on the bread and the wine themselves, he treats the Lord's Supper in connection with the feeding of the 5,000 rather than in relation to the Last Supper in the Upper Room. In a similar way he presents Jesus himself as the "bread of life" which comes from heaven and gives life to the world (6:33-35, 48-51). Jesus not only gives bread, but he is himself the bread from heaven. Jesus fulfills the Jewish expectation that the Messiah will once again bring manna from heaven (Midr. Eccles. 1, 9, 9b), but at the same time he transposes this expectation into a higher key.

By focusing on Jesus himself, rather than the elements of bread and wine, John wishes to indicate that the material elements of the sacrament, in the final analysis, having meaning only because of the incarnation of the Son of God. In this vein John also suggests that the Christian observance of the Lord's Supper recalls the entire earthly life of Jesus, including his incarnation (6:33, 51) and the activities of his ministry (6:26, 38) as well as his death (6:51). Throughout his presentation, finally, John stresses the central importance of hearing the words of life that Jesus speaks (6:63, 68) and believing in him (6:29, 35, 36, 40, 47, 64, 69). Only in this context of hearing and believing does John affirm that eternal life comes from the food which Jesus gives (6:27, 33, 35, 48, 50-51, 53-58). By calling attention to these aspects of Christian sacramental observance, John may well intend to avoid any *ex opere operato* understanding of the Lord's Supper. At the same time, his emphasis on "hearing" and "believing" reflects the importance that he attaches to the relationship between Jesus and the believer as the context for an appropriate interpretation of the Lord's Supper.

In depicting Jesus as the bread of life, John divides his narrative into six scenes, consisting of two incidents and then four passages of discourse or dialogue. The feeding of the 5,000 (6:1-15) is followed directly by the incident in which Jesus walks on the water (6:16-21). Then Jesus speaks to "the crowd" that had shared in the feeding (6:25-40), to "the Jews" (6:41-59), to "many of his disciples" (6:60-65), and to "the twelve" (6:66-71). The distinctions among these four groups are not entirely clear, since "the crowd" were presumably Jewish, "the Jews" had acquired some knowledge of the feeding of the 5,000, "many of his disciples" were presumably included in the crowd, and "the twelve" were among his disciples generally. The indistinct lines of demarcation among the four groups suggest that John perceives them less as separate classes of people than as ways of responding to Jesus and entering into relation with him as the bread of life.

The feeding of the 5,000 is the only miracle narrative related in all four gospels. In Matthew and Mark it is followed directly by the incident of walking on the water, an event that Luke omits. John may have combined the feeding and the walking on water because they were already linked together in the tradition that he received. At the same time, however, he finds the latter passage useful in supporting his portrayal of Jesus as the bread of life. As Jesus draws near to the disciples in the boat, he says, "It is I; do not be afraid" (6:20). The words "it is I" (*egō eimi*, literally "I am") serve to identify him to the disciples, but also, as an echo of Yahweh's "I am He" in Second Isaiah, they convey the awesome majesty of his divine nature.[22] John indicates in this way that Jesus, who feeds the 5,000 and offers life to the world, can never be seen as less than the divine Son of God himself.

After these two events, the feeding and the walking on water, John presents Jesus' first discourse, directed to "the crowd" that had eaten their "fill of the loaves" (6:26). The discourse deals with important topics that people would ask about as they reflect on the significance of the feeding. It points out, for example, that real food is not ordinary loaves of bread but "the food that endures for eternal life" (6:27); the "work" of God is "that you believe in him whom he has sent" (6:29); the "sign" which Jesus gives is himself, since he is the bread of God "which comes down from heaven and gives life to the world" (6:33); the "will" of God is that "all who see the Son and believe in him may have eternal life" (6:40). The reaction to the feeding is incomplete, John suggests, until people can understand it in terms such as these. Although the members of "the crowd" seem to be generally receptive to Jesus, they need help in understanding more fully the meaning of the event in which they have shared.

In the following discourses or dialogues John draws attention to other issues that are involved in understanding Jesus as the bread of life. The second discourse is addressed to "the Jews," who are puzzled or offended by the idea that the earthly Jesus, whom they think they know, can be the bread of life that comes down from heaven and gives his own life for the life of the world. The third discourse is given to "many of his disciples," who, like the Jews, are puzzled or offended by the thought of eating flesh and drinking blood. Finally, in a fourth passage, Jesus converses briefly with "the twelve" to test the firmness of their faith. Peter, probably as representative of the group, affirms that there is no one else to whom they can go.

The fact that John delineates these four groups of people without sharply differentiating them from one another suggests that they represent a variety of responses that people can make to Jesus as the bread of life -- not only those who were originally reacting to Jesus after the feeding of the 5,000, but also Christian believers within the church as they engage in the ongoing process of understanding Jesus and believing in him. Life within the community, John suggests, does not rest simply on a static, one-dimensional affirmation of faith. It involves change, growth, and reaffirmation, as believers involve themselves in the process of deepening and enriching their understanding and faith.

From this point of view, Christians within the community of faith can react in different ways to Jesus as the bread of life, corresponding to the groups of people depicted in connection with the feeding of the 5,000. Like "the crowd," they can be receptive to Jesus' ministry and interested in learning more about him. Like "the Jews," they can be puzzled or even offended at the idea that the earthly Jesus is the incarnate Son who came from heaven and gives eternal life. Like the "disciples," they need to realize that it is the spirit that gives life, not the material elements of bread and wine in themselves. Like the "twelve," they always need, too, to join in Peter's confession that Jesus alone has the words of eternal life.

Life within the community of faith thus means that believers can divide themselves into different groups, according to the type of response they make to Jesus, the depth of their understanding, or the maturity of their faith. Individual believers may find themselves in more than one group at a time, or they may go from one group to another as they deal with different issues or make different responses to Jesus. Believers may relate to one another as members of these rather indistinct groups, as well as through their membership in the community as a whole. Relationships among believers become complex, as one form of relationship must be correlated with another and sometimes priorities must be established. Much as people originally reacted in different ways to Jesus' feeding of the 5,000, so believers may find themselves in different segments of the community of faith as they arrive at particular stages of growth or specific formulations of faith.

John would not want to suggest that the community of faith is an amorphous aggregation of individual believers in which one type of faith is as authentic as any other. He does, indeed, recognize that believers are *in via*, engaged in an ongoing process of spiritual growth, and he acknowledges too that individual persons may ask different questions or arrive at particular stages of growth at different times. John wishes, at the same time, to establish hermeneutical control over the concept that people may divide themselves into groups as they respond in various ways to Jesus in his role as the bread of life. John insists, for example, that believers seek to understand their faith by asking serious and apposite questions about Jesus as he functions in this role. They need to ask about issues such as the relation between the bread that Jesus gives and the bread that he is, or the relation between matter and spirit as aspects of the elements in the Lord's Supper.

John also indicates, in a similar way, that stages of spiritual growth and understanding must always be controlled by a recognition of the uniqueness of Jesus as the only true bread of life. If they are to engage in a meaningful process of growth, and if they are to appreciate the position of others in the community who have arrived at different stages of growth, believers must always be able to profess, with Peter, that Jesus alone has the words of eternal life. This kind of affirmation provides a basis of unity for the community of faith and functions at the same time as a criterion for assessing the authenticity of the diverse ways of understanding Jesus as people respond to him and arrive at various stages of spiritual growth.

In delineating different types of response that people make to Jesus within the text, John is also pointing out possible ways that readers may respond in reading and actualizing the text. In establishing hermeneutical control over responses within the text, John is also indicating that readers must adhere to certain procedures and norms as they come into engagement with the text. In both instances John gives models within the text for the types of response that readers may make to the text. These models of response become one of the most important narrative techniques by which John recognizes the need for readers to respond to the text at the same time that he indicates appropriate directions for their responses to take.

C. One Flock: Jews and Gentiles

The first part of Chapter 10, in which John presents Jesus as "the good shepherd" (10:14), seems to have the same setting as the preceding chapters. Chapters 7-9 were placed at the festival of Tabernacles, held in the month of October (7:2, 10, 14, 37). Chapter 10:1-21 seems to have this setting also, since 10:21 gives a clear reference to the healing of the blind man in Chapter 9. In the second part of Chapter 10, beginning with 10:22, the time changes to the feast of Dedication, or Hanukkah, which was celebrated in December. It is possible that the mention of Dedication in 10:22 is intended to provide a temporal setting for the entire chapter. It is more likely, however, that John simply wished to indicate at 10:22 that several months had now passed by.

In Chapter 10, John uses a literary style that does not correspond exactly to the forms of speech in the Synoptics. He describes it in 10:6 as a "figure of speech" (*paroimia*), but his writing at this point lacks the concise action of a parable or the detailed narration of an allegory. Action, in the strict sense, is replaced by general statements referring to action. In this chapter, John is painting a picture rather than telling a story. Through symbols such as shepherd, sheepfold, and sheep, he seeks to construct a sustained image that presents important aspects of the work of Jesus and depicts the relationships that form the context for Jesus' work.

From the standpoint of relation analysis, it is significant that John depicts a rich variety of relationships involving God the Father, Jesus, and Christian believers. John indicates, for example, that Jesus stands in the closest possible, ongoing relation with the Father -- the Father knows Jesus, and Jesus knows the Father (10:15); the Father loves Jesus (10:17); the Father is in Jesus, and Jesus is in the Father (10:38); Jesus and the Father are "one," or a "unity" (*hen*, 10:30).

In a similar way John delineates the relationship between Jesus and believers, with special emphasis here on Jesus' redemptive action on behalf of believers -- Jesus is the shepherd of the sheep (10:2, 11, 14, 26-29) and the door to the sheepfold (10:7, 9); he knows his own, and his own know him (10:14); he voluntarily lays down his life for the sheep (10:11, 15, 17-18); he gives salvation (10:9), life abundant (10:10), and life eternal (10:28).

There is a close connection between Jesus' relationship to the Father and his relationship to believers. As the Father knows Jesus and Jesus knows the Father, so Jesus knows his own and his own know him (10:14-15). The closeness of the first relationship provides a measure for the closeness of the second. Also, the Father loves Jesus because he voluntarily gives his life for believers (10:17-18). Although, presumably, the Father would love the Son for other reasons as well, or for no reason other than his own loving nature, John wishes to indicate here that the Father is fully aware of, and responsive to, the sacrificial service of the Son. In this respect Jesus' relationship to believers actually has an effect on his relationship to the Father. Jesus is related to the Father, finally, in the sense that he and the Father have parallel relationships to believers: no one can "snatch" them out of the "hand" of either Jesus or the Father (10:27-30). Whether one relationship provides a measure for the second, or is affected by the second, or is parallel to the second, John wishes to delineate the close inter-connection between Jesus' relationship to the Father and his relationship to believers. Neither one, John implies, can be seen in isolation from the other.

In presenting Jesus as the good shepherd, John seeks to emphasize the work of Jesus on behalf of believers and the continuing nature of his relation to them. At the same time, it is significant that John also utilizes this chapter to depict the relationship of believers to one another within the new community of faith. Some believers, for example, are of Jewish background. From the "sheepfold" of the covenant people of Israel, they hear the voice of Jesus calling them, and they choose to follow him (10:3-4). Some believers, on the other hand, are of Gentile background. They do not belong to the "fold" of Judaism, but Jesus has come to call them also (10:16a). Both groups of believers will enter the new Christian community, and "there will be one flock, one shepherd" (10:16b; cf. 10:27).

This union of Jews and Gentiles into a new community must have been an established fact by the time John wrote, since he records it without comment and seems to accept it as a natural, logical result of Jesus' redemptive work. Nor does John try to indicate to what extent Jews and Gentiles could preserve their own heritages within the Christian community. He does not seem interested in addressing this issue, possibly because it had already become clear by his own time that all Christian believers, of whatever background, should measure their beliefs and practices by the criterion of faith in Jesus as incarnate Son and Redeemer. For the time and place in which he was writing, John seems to have considered it sufficient to indicate that the new Christian community did indeed include people of both Jewish and Gentile background.

If John seems rather casual in writing about the inclusion of Jews and Gentiles in the church, the method of relation analysis helps to delineate the setting in which he depicts this event. The importance of the setting, in turn, suggests that John regarded the event as highly significant. The relationships between the Father and the Son, and the Son and believers, are important in themselves, but are also significant because they underlie the relationships of believers to one another in the community of faith. Thus Jews and Gentiles do not simply form a new unity in the church because they have similar ideas about religion. Both are "sheep" -- i.e., both know the voice of their shepherd and follow him (10:4, 16, 27), both receive eternal life from Jesus (10:10, 28), both share in the benefit of his vicarious death (10:11, 15, 17-18). It is Jesus' relationship to believers that brings them together from diverse backgrounds into the community of faith, and this relationship in turn reflects his own relationship with the Father.

This context or network of relationships in which Jews and Gentiles enter the new community of faith has several further implications for John's understanding of the church. It signifies, for example, that the basis of unity in the church is theological and soteriological, rather than cultural and anthropological. Whatever background people in the church may have, and whatever cultural patterns they would regard as compatible with their faith, they receive the opportunity to be believers, in the final analysis, only because of Jesus' relationship to the Father and his relationship to believers. Jews and Gentiles, further, are equal within the church, for they enter it on the same basis of "hearing" and "following" the call that Jesus gives, even though, from a historical perspective, John can write elsewhere that "salvation is from the Jews" (4:22). Whatever background people in the church have, they are also equal within the community of faith because they all enter it on the basis of God's grace rather than their own accomplishment. Jews and Gentiles, finally, now receive a new spiritual heritage, consisting of the relationships that John has delineated so carefully among God the Father, Jesus, and believers. If people wish to be Christian, John suggests, they need to understand that they are believing in the Father who is related to Jesus, and Jesus who is related to believers. These relationships constitute a new spiritual heritage that now governs the faith and actions of believers, even though, in a historical sense, John would not wish to minimize the importance of the Jewish background to Christianity.

To delineate these significant aspects of the Christian community, John utilizes the technique of correlating relationships with one another. The relation of the Father to the Son is parallel in several respects to the relation of Jesus to believers, and this relation in turn underlies the relationship of believers to one another within the community of faith. John wants the reader to perceive, in effect, that affirming the ideology of the text means accepting membership in a community of faith, and this acceptance in turn involves recognition and affirmation of the network of relationships in which the community originates.

John also uses the technique of omission, or gaps in the text, as a way of calling the reader's attention to important aspects of any response that the reader decides to make to the text. Whether the reader comes from a Jewish or a Gentile background, it is significant that John does not try to specify which religious or cultural aspects of that background would still be acceptable in Christianity, or how the old background can be related to the new spiritual heritage that people receive as members of the new community of faith. John wants the reader to recognize that these issues need to be addressed in light of faith in Jesus as incarnate Word, Lord, and Savior. The reader, John believes, must undertake this process of critical reflection as part of any attempt to read and actualize the text.

D. Last Supper and Lord's Supper

Chapter 13 may be regarded as the beginning of the second major part of the Gospel of John. Up to this point John has depicted the public ministry of Jesus in Galilee and Judea. Even in Chapter 12, which forms a transitional link between the two halves of the gospel, John has presented events, such as the "triumphal entry" into Jerusalem, which have a public setting. Now, beginning with Chapter 13, John will describe the last few hours of Jesus' life on earth. Events during this period will include the Last Supper, the "Farewell Discourses" to the disciples, Jesus' prayer to the Father, his arrest, trial, crucifixion, and resurrection.

The account of the Last Supper in Chapter 13 thus has a prominent position at the beginning of the second major part of the gospel. This position probably reflects the historical sequence of events, since in synoptic tradition also the public ministry of Jesus completely precedes the account of the Last Supper. At the same time, it is very likely that John gives special prominence to the Last Supper because it introduces the series of chapters in which he is especially concerned with the meaning of discipleship and the nature of the Christian community. Throughout this section he is thinking not only of Jesus' final hours with his disciples, but also of the ongoing Christian community that has its basis in the life and work of the historical Jesus. Thus the Last Supper becomes a paradigm for understanding the significance of the Lord's Supper, and Jesus' farewell discourses to his disciples become a major part of his teaching to all Christian believers.

The methodology of relation analysis helps to delineate the distinctive features of John's account of the Last Supper, especially when his account is compared with those in the Synoptics. The writers of the synoptic gospels are not explicitly concerned at this point with the relationship between God and Jesus; they evidently assume its existence and importance, but they perceive no particular need to refer to it in this setting (Matt. 26:20-29; Mk. 14:17-25; Lk. 22:14-19a). In a similar way, apart from an occasional phrase such as "with you" (Matt. 26:29; Lk. 22:15) or, in the longer text of Luke, "for you" (Lk. 22:19b-20), the writers of the Synoptics put no explicit emphasis on Jesus' relation to the disciples. They assume that Jesus is doing something of paramount importance for the disciples, but in their narratives they focus attention almost completely on the actions and words of Jesus himself.

John, in contrast, is clearly interested in presenting the relationships that constitute the setting for his account of the Last Supper. At the beginning of his account he emphasizes the relation between Jesus and the Father, not simply as an introduction to the account but as the context in which the Last Supper will take place:

> ... Jesus knew that his hour had come to depart from this world and go to the Father. (13:1)

> Jesus, knowing that the Father had given all things into his hands, and that he had come from God and was going to God... (13:3)

Following his description of the footwashing, John explains its significance by referring once again to relationships -- this time the relation between Jesus and the disciples, and the relation of the disciples to one

another. He stresses the proportional connection between these two
relationships:

> So if I, your Lord and Teacher, have washed your feet,
> you also ought to wash one another's feet. For I have set you
> an example, that you also should do as I have done to you.
> (13:14-15)

Shortly afterward, John refers to all these relationships again, stating
them this time in chiastic order: the relation of believers to believers, of
believers to Jesus, and of Jesus to the Father all appear within the scope of
one verse:

> Very truly, I tell you, whoever receives one whom I send
> receives me; and whoever receives me receives him who sent
> me. (13:20)

John's treatment of the glorification of Jesus reflects the relationship
between Jesus and God, since God himself is glorified in the glorification of
Jesus as Son of man (13:31-32). Finally, John's presentation of the "new
commandment" is formulated in terms of the proportional relationships that
exist between Jesus and the disciples, and the disciples with one another:

> I give you a new commandment, that you love one
> another. Just as I have loved you, you also should love one
> another. By this everyone will know that you are my disciples,
> if you have love for one another. (13:34-35; cf. 15:12-13).

By delineating these relationships so carefully, John establishes the
setting which he regards as essential for his presentation of the events and
themes of Chapter 13, such as the footwashing, the idea of being glorified,
and the new commandment of love for one another. Without this setting,
John implies, the meaning of these aspects of the Last Supper could not be
fully appreciated. In this way John calls attention to the interpretive
significance of relationships that has no parallel in the corresponding
accounts in the synoptic gospels.

John also presents the relationships themselves in a sequence which
illustrates how one relationship underlies another. To introduce the chapter,
and to establish the setting for the further development of its themes, John

speaks first of the relation between the Father and Jesus (13:1, 3). This relationship in turn makes it possible to speak of the one between Jesus and the disciples, which then becomes the paradigm for the relation of the disciples to one another (13:14-15, 34-35). Although John often speaks of these three relationships throughout his gospel, it is perhaps in Chapter 13 that he indicates most clearly how one relationship underlies, and gives form and content to, another. Here again, John reflects an appreciation for the critical importance of relationships that has no parallel in the synoptic accounts of the Last Supper.

John's own account of the Last Supper focuses on Jesus' action of washing the feet of the disciples (13:2-11). John relates this event at approximately the same point at which the Synoptics give the "words of explanation" concerning the bread and the wine (e.g., "this is my body... this is my blood...," Mk. 14:22, 24) and also the "eschatological pronouncement" ("Truly, I tell you, I will never again drink of the fruit of the vine until that day when I drink it new in the kingdom of God," Mk. 14:25). John omits both the words of explanation and the eschatological pronouncement; indeed, he makes no specific mention of the bread and the wine, indicating only that the footwashing occurred "during supper" (13:2). Whether John is intentionally revising synoptic tradition at this point, or whether he is only following his own sources, he clearly wishes to emphasize the significance of the footwashing. It is also significant that he wishes, in general, to place his account of the Last Supper within a context that is relational rather than eschatological.

In several ways John indicates that he understands the footwashing in close conjunction with the sacrificial death of Jesus, which is only hours away. In the first verse, which is programmatic for the entire chapter, he notes that Jesus was anticipating his death: "Jesus knew that his hour had come to depart from this world and go to the Father" (13:1; cf. 13:3). In a manner that is characteristic of his style, John develops his thought by using a phrase with a double meaning: "Having loved his own who were in the world, he loved them to the end (*eis telos*)" (13:1). This phrase can have a temporal meaning ("to the end of his life") and also a qualitative significance ("to the utmost, fully, completely"). Together these meanings signify that Jesus, by dying on behalf of others, gave the fullest possible expression of his love for them. Thus at the beginning of the chapter, before he actually describes the footwashing, John establishes a close connection with the imminent death of Jesus.

Following his account of the footwashing, John refers again to Jesus' death when he notes that "the Son of Man has been glorified (*edoxasthē*)" (13:31). Jesus is glorified by his return to the Father -- a continuous upward movement that includes the events of death, resurrection, and ascension. Through the literary device of the "dramatic aorist," John uses a past tense to depict this imminent glorification of Jesus; the event is so real to him that he can write of it as if it had already happened. In a similar way John uses the dramatic aorist in writing of Jesus' new commandment: "Just as I have loved (*ēgapēsa*) you," Jesus explains, "you also should love one another" (13:34). Because Jesus loved his disciples to the point of dying on their behalf, John can refer to Jesus' imminent death by using the verb "love" in the past tense.

By his references to Jesus' death, and through the literary devices of double meaning and dramatic aorist, John makes it clear that he perceives the footwashing in close connection with Jesus' death. In both instances Jesus acts voluntarily and intentionally, and in both instances he performs an action on behalf of the disciples, making known his love for them. The first event points toward the second, with a connection so close that the footwashing, for John, seems to become a preenactment of Jesus' sacrificial death on the cross.

In the footwashing scene, John includes a conversation between Jesus and Peter to indicate that the new Christian community, in the final analysis, has its basis in Jesus' sacrificial love for the disciples. When Peter demurs at the thought that Jesus would wash his feet, Jesus replies, "Unless I wash you, you have no share with me" (13:8). Since the footwashing anticipates the sacrificial death of Jesus, the meaning here seems to be that Jesus' death on behalf of the disciples is essential in order that the new Christian community may come into being. Christians, therefore, are people who have received the benefits of Jesus' sacrificial death. On this basis then they interact with one another, seeking to love one another as Jesus loved them (13:34-35). In terms of relation analysis, the relationship that Jesus establishes with believers brings the Christian community into being; the relationship of believers to one another is modeled after the relation that Jesus has established with them -- it is proportional to it, is a way of responding to it, and becomes a way, finally, of maintaining the vitality of the Christian community.

John continues the conversation between Jesus and Peter to indicate that Jesus' death is sufficient in itself to provide the basis for the new community of believers. It represents an act of love so complete that it does not need to be supplemented by other actions on his part. Peter, not understanding this, asks that his hands and his head may be washed as well as his feet (13:9). Jesus assures Peter, in effect, that washing his feet is enough, since it represents proleptically his own sacrificial death that is sufficient and more than sufficient for bringing the new community into being (13:10). The relationship that Jesus is establishing with believers is not only necessary, but also sufficient, as a basis for their relationship with one another.

Along with the Synoptics, John treats the theme of Judas' betrayal of Jesus in connection with the Last Supper. The Synoptics introduce this theme with a preliminary note before the Last Supper itself takes place (Matt. 26:14-16; Mk. 14:10-11; Lk. 22:3-6). Then they include Jesus' prediction of the betrayal as part of their account of the Last Supper, apparently near the beginning of the meal (Matt. 26:21-25; Mk. 14:18-21) or following the actual meal (Lk. 22:21-23). John links the theme of the betrayal even more closely with the Last Supper. He introduces the theme in the setting of the Last Supper itself (13:2), mentions it again following the footwashing (13:10-11, 18-19), and then gives it a lengthy narrative development (13:21-30). In this way John presents the idea of the betrayal of Jesus as a major theme of the chapter, using it especially to bracket his account of the footwashing (13:3-10).

Why is John concerned to link the theme of betrayal so closely with his account of the Last Supper? The Synoptics also reflect this connection, which may well be historical, but John establishes it even more firmly. John may wish to give special emphasis to the fact that Judas, one of the twelve, participated in the Last Supper and presumably had his feet washed by Jesus, yet he still betrayed Jesus. His participation in the Last Supper, that is, did not automatically ensure that he would be loyal to his Master. Even the footwashing, as a symbol of the sacrificial significance of Jesus' imminent death, did not result in an *ipso facto* guarantee of loyalty.

In a similar way, viewing the Last Supper as the basis for the continuing rite of the Lord's Supper in the church, John wishes to indicate that reception of the sacrament does not automatically ensure faith and loyalty on the part of believers. The sacrament of the Lord's Supper does indeed become a channel for the communication of divine grace. At the same time, however, believers need to respond to God's grace by acknowledging Jesus as Teacher and Lord (13:13) and by showing love to one another (13:34-35). It is interesting that these two responses -- toward Jesus and toward one another -- are approximately parallel to the structure of the Ten Commandments in the Old Testament, which deal first with the people's relationship to God (Ex. 20:3-11) and then with their relationship with one another (Ex. 20:12-17). Intentionally or not, John reflects this basic perspective of biblical thought in delineating the responses that believers should make to God's grace.

It is perhaps a moot point whether, in John's view, believers would actually receive divine grace from the sacrament even without making the appropriate response, or whether they would have grace available to them from the sacrament but would appropriate it only through their spiritual and ethical response. This issue concerning God's grace is analogous to the question concerning God's forgiveness, as it is presented in Matthew's parable of the unmerciful servant (Matt. 18:23-35). This parable suggests that God makes his forgiveness available on his own initiative, prior to any human action, but then it emphasizes that people can appropriate divine forgiveness only by offering forgiveness in turn to their fellow human beings.[23] Whether or not John thinks in a similar way about the divine grace that the sacrament offers, he clearly wishes to underline the importance of appropriate response on the part of Christian believers.

In terms of relation analysis, John's emphasis on the need for appropriate response to God's grace indicates that the sacramental life of the Christian community is intrinsically connected to the fabric of the continuing relationships that people sustain with their Lord and with one another. It is not as if sacraments represent one sphere of the community's life, and relationships another, so that people would move from one to the other without discerning any connection between them. Nor do "sacraments" and "fellowship" represent two distinct foci of Christian life, or two distinct areas of Christian experience, tending to attract different groups of people. It is important to perceive, John indicates, that God's grace in the sacrament always requires a response on the part of believers, and this response finds expression through relationships with other personal beings. In this respect, participation in the sacramental life of the community has the effect of strengthening and enriching the relationships that believers have with their Lord and with one another.

When Judas leaves the scene of the Last Supper to carry out his betrayal of Jesus, John makes the brief, poignant comment, "And it was night" (13:30). The term "night" starkly contrasts Judas with Jesus, who is the light of the world (8:12; 9:5; 12:35). It also serves to contrast the actions of Judas with the way of life followed by true disciples, who are not to walk in darkness (8:12) but to work while it is day (9:4) and believe in the light so that they may become "children of light" (12:36). These contrasts also illustrate how pervasively John is thinking in terms of relationships in his presentation of the Last Supper. Judas, who leaves the scene at night, represents at this point the complete absence of any relationship with Jesus; the disciples, working in the day and believing in the light, are to symbolize the meaning of positive, continuing, faithful relationship with Jesus.

Whereas John uses the theme of the betrayal by Judas to highlight the need for believers to make an appropriate response to God's grace, he utilizes the prediction of Peter's denial of Jesus to point to the consequences that faithful discipleship may entail. Here again John puts his own stamp on a motif that had appeared in synoptic tradition. He does this partly by connecting the prediction very closely with the meal itself, placing it immediately after the "new commandment" passage and indicating that he is still thinking at this point of ways of responding to God's grace. Just as the disciples in general should show love for one another (13:34-35), so Peter in particular should remain faithful to Jesus (13:36-38). The Synoptics do not reflect this close connection between the Last Supper and Jesus' prediction that Peter will deny him. Matthew and Mark place the prediction after the meal, when Jesus and his disciples have gone to the Mount of Olives (Matt. 26:33-35; Mk. 14:29-31). Luke is closer to John at this point, placing the prediction near the end of the "table talk" that he includes following the meal (Lk. 22:31-34).

John also formulates the prediction itself with a distinctive wording that makes it not only a prediction of Peter's denial of Jesus, but also a prediction of Peter's death at a later time. "Where I am going," Jesus says to Peter, "you cannot follow me now; but you will follow afterward" (13:36). Although the synoptic passages refer to the possibility of Peter's death, they envision a situation in which he may die at the same time as Jesus (Matt. 26:35; Mk. 14:31; Lk. 22:33). If Peter actually died in A.D. 64 or 65, it is very possible that all four gospel writers were aware of his death. Only John, however, reflects such an awareness at this point. John has modified the prediction of Peter's denial so that the emphasis falls as much on Peter's own death as on the denial itself.

From the standpoint of relation analysis, it appears that John is still thinking at this point in terms of the responses that believers make to God's grace. The footwashing represents the theme of divine grace, given expression through Jesus' love for the disciples and his sacrificial death on the cross. The disciples in general are to respond by acknowledging Jesus as Teacher and Lord (13:13) and by loving one another (13:34-35). Through these responses they sustain their all-important relationships with Jesus and with one another. As a particular case, Judas represents negative response, with ensuing loss of relationship; neither the disciples nor Jesus, according to John, ever speaks to Judas again. As another particular case, and in contrast to Judas, Peter represents a mixed kind of response that begins with denial of Jesus but eventually leads to faithful discipleship and even martyrdom for his faith. Although John does not pass over the denial, he prefers to look at Peter's life as a whole, emphasizing his career of faithful response and loyal discipleship.

In contrast to the synoptic accounts of the Last Supper, John's account emphasizes the significance of relationships as the setting in which events take place and their meaning is to be perceived. In a manner that is completely absent from the synoptic accounts, John explicitly calls attention to the relationships involving the Father and Jesus, Jesus and the disciples, and the disciples with one another. By way of summary, it will be helpful to look at three reasons why John is so concerned to delineate this relational context for his own presentation of the events of the Last Supper.

The careful attention to relationships, first, supports the view that John regards the Last Supper as a model for the church's continuing rite of observing the Lord's Supper. In describing the Last Supper, John is also thinking of the Lord's Supper; and in depicting the actions of the original disciples, he is also thinking of later Christian believers. The relationships involving God, Jesus, and believers carry over from one setting to the other, so that they continue to characterize the life of the Christian community. This continuity of relationships, for John, provides an organic connection between the past and the present.

Secondly, John's concern for the relational setting of Chapter 13 reflects his conviction that the Christian community has its origin in divine action, expressed in the context of the relationships between the Father and the Son, and between the Son and believers. The Christian community is not simply a group of people with similar religious, cultural, or social backgrounds. It is not even, in the first instance, a group of people who hold similar beliefs, in spite of the importance of the concept of "believing" for John. The Christian community has its origin and continuing basis in the Father's action of sending the Son and in the Son's ministry and death on behalf of believers.

A third reason why John emphasizes the relational setting in his account of the Last Supper is that he wishes to underline the need for the disciples to make an appropriate response to Jesus' words and deeds. In general terms, John indicates that the disciples need to respond by believing in Jesus as Teacher and Lord, and by obeying the commandment to love one another. But then the prominence that John gives to Judas and Peter in this chapter illustrates further his concern for the nature of the response that believers make. Only through a suitable response, John suggests, can believers cultivate and sustain their relationships with God, Jesus, and one another -- relationships that derive ultimately from the gift of divine grace.

In his account of the Lord's Supper, John uses several techniques to construct the narrative world to which the reader must respond. Whether or not he assumes that the reader is familiar with synoptic tradition at this point, John clearly wishes to place his own account within the interpretive context of relationships involving the Father, the Son, and believers. He wants the reader to be aware that actualizing the text of the Last Supper means recognizing and accepting the relationships that the occasion illustrates. John also correlates these relationships with one another, showing how one underlies another, and he emphasizes the need for ethical response to divine grace. As a strategy for guiding the reader's response at this point, John gives examples within the text of the ways people may respond to Jesus, highlighting in particular the contrast between Judas and Peter.

E. Love within the Christian Community

The analysis of the theme of love in Chapter I focused on the love that the Father shows to the Son. The analysis in Chapter II emphasized God's love for believers, with some attention to other facets that John depicts, such as Jesus' own love for believers and the believers' love for Jesus. In both of these chapters the study of the theme of love showed especially that John thinks of love as a dynamic love that expresses itself in some action that benefits the recipient. The treatment in these chapters also called attention to other aspects of love, such as the paradox that it can be unconditional and also contingent. Both chapters suggested that John regards love as a major theme in his understanding of the relationships within the Godhead and between God and believers.

In contrast to his extensive treatment of love in these other relationships, John says relatively little about love within the Christian community. He adumbrates the theme in the footwashing at the Last Supper, when Jesus says to the disciples, "So if I, your Lord and Teacher, have washed your feet, you also ought to wash one another's feet. For I have set you an example, that you also should do as I have done to you" (13:14-15). Then, shortly afterward, John states the love commandment directly, as part of Jesus' discourse at the close of the supper: "I give you a new commandment, that you love one another. Just as I have loved you, you also should love one another" (13:34). It is significant here that Jesus' own love for his followers becomes the model for the love that they are to show to one another. His own love is a self-sacrificial love, even to the point of giving his life for them. Jesus' words, "I have loved" (*egapēsa*), can be understood as a "dramatic aorist," which expresses a coming event -- his death on the cross -- as if it had already taken place.

John gives the love commandment again in 15:12-13, bringing out the connection once more between Jesus' love for the disciples and his death on their behalf, and presenting Jesus' love once more as the paradigm for the love that the disciples should show to one another. Finally, John summarizes the commandment briefly in 15:17. These references are the only ones that John makes to the practice of love within the Christian community. He places them all in the setting of the Last Supper and the Farewell Discourses, in which Jesus is giving his disciples instruction for their continuing life as a community following his own departure from their midst.

In view of John's very limited treatment of love within the Christian community, it becomes all the more important, in terms of relation analysis, to identify the relationships that form the setting in which he presents this theme. Two of these are especially significant. First, as the Father has loved the Son, so the Son has loved the disciples (15:9). Then, in turn, as the Son has loved the disciples, so they are to love one another (13:34). In developing the theme of love, John's thought begins with the Father's relation to the Son, then moves to the Son's relation to the disciples, and finally comes to the disciples' relation to one another. Each relationship forms the context and establishes the norm for those that follow, as John indicates by using words like "as" and "so," or "just as" and "also." John's understanding of love within the community of believers, therefore, must be analogous to the forms of love that he has presented in the relationships involving the Father, the Son, and the disciples.

As John delineates the nature of love in these other relationships, he presents it as an active and dynamic love, concerned with promoting the best interests and enhancing the well-being of its object. The Father, for example, loves the Son and has given all things to him (3:35); God loved the world and gave his Son to the world (3:16); the Son loves the disciples and lays down his life for them (15:13). In each instance, love expresses itself in an action on behalf of its object, even though the action may be costly to the subject.

In a similar way, since John thinks of one relationship as giving structure and content to another, it is very likely that he thinks of love within the Christian community as an active, self-giving love that always seeks to benefit its object. When Jesus commanded the disciples to love one another as he loved them (13:34; 15:12), he was thinking, as John understands it, of this active form of love. It is consistent with this understanding of love that Jesus' commandment of love in the Christian community (15:12) is followed directly by his reference to his own self-sacrifice on behalf of the disciples (15:13).

When Jesus gives the "new commandment" to the disciples, he presents his own love for them as an example: "I give you a new commandment, that you love one another. Just as I have loved you, you also should love one another" (13:34). It is Jesus' reference to his own example that makes this a "new" commandment. John was presumably familiar with the traditional commandment, "You shall love your neighbor as yourself," as he would have found it in the Old Testament (Lev. 19:18), if not in Jesus' teachings preserved in synoptic tradition (cf. Matt. 5:43; 19:19; 22:39; Mk. 12:31; Lk. 10:27). John evidently felt, however, that this love for neighbor, based on a person's natural tendency to value himself or herself as a person, needed to be transposed into a more dynamic love for others that would be patterned after Jesus' own sacrificial love. Although John did not necessarily object to the traditional commandment of love for neighbor, he believed that the theme of love should be understood relationally-i.e., believers should love one another with the type of love with which Jesus loved them.

When John records Jesus' teaching about love, he never indicates that Jesus instructed his followers to love all people, or the "world" generally. Unlike Paul, who encouraged the Christians in Thessalonica to "abound in love for one another and for all" (I Thess. 3:12; cf. Gal. 6:10), John gives only the teaching that the disciples should love one another. In this respect there would appear to be an "in-group limitation" in the understanding of love in the Fourth Gospel, as if love were to be shown only to other members of the Christian community and not to those outside.

In one sense this limitation does exist, since love for one another is to be a hallmark of the Christian community. As Jesus instructs his followers, "By this everyone will know that you are my disciples, if you have love for one another" (13:35). Although Jesus' words do not necessarily mean that the disciples should not show love to those outside the community, they do emphasize that the active, dynamic love that seeks the well-being of others should become a distinguishing feature of the emerging Christian fellowship. If there is an "in-group limitation" in John's presentation of Christian love, the limitation does have a positive function in encouraging the practice of love as an essential part of the life of the community.

John's understanding of the "world," which will be examined more fully in Chapter IV, also helps to explain the restrictions that he evidently places on the scope of Christian love. John can use the term "world" to designate the material and human world that results from God's creative activity. He can also use the term to represent human society, as it formulates its own standards and values and rejects those of Christian faith. To the extent that the world represents human society as it rejects Jesus (1:10c), the followers of Jesus can not love the world. Like Jesus himself, they can not belong to the world (17:14, 16) or affirm its values (15:19).

Since God himself loves the world and seeks to embrace it within the scope of his salvation (3:16-17), it would seem consistent with the relational quality of John's thought that the disciples of Jesus can reflect God's love for the world and relate positively to the world, at least in the sense of making known the love that God has shown. God's own love establishes a relationship to the world in which believers can share and within which they can legitimately function as believers. In this respect believers can be sent into the world with a mission to the world. As the Father sent the Son into the world, John notes, so the Son sends his followers into the world (17:18).

Since John never states explicitly that believers are to love the world, it is possible that he wishes to make a fine distinction between actually loving the world and communicating God's own love for the world. Believers can not love the world themselves because they do not belong to the world and they can not support its values. Yet, as those whom Jesus sent into the world, they have the very important task of communicating, to the world, God's love for the world. In this respect John may wish to indicate that the dialectic of Christian existence has its basis, not only in a temporal distinction between an "already" and a "not yet," but also in an existential attitude that must differentiate between loving the world *per se* and communicating, in whatever way is most appropriate, the continuing validity of God's own love for the world.

In his treatment of love within the Christian community, John draws the reader's attention to the way one relationship underlies another -- the relation of the Father to the Son underlies the relation of Jesus to his followers, and this in turn underlies the relation of believers to one another. John wants the reader to become aware of a narrative world in which "loving one another" is more than simply obedience to a commandment; it is the result of a sequence in which one relationship has provided the basis and norm for another. John also establishes a gap in his presentation by omitting any commandment for believers to love the world generally. In this way he encourages the reader to think carefully about the relation of believers to the world. In particular, John invites the reader to consider ways in which believers, without having a direct command to love the world, may share in, or reflect, God's own love for the world. By correlating relationships with one another, and by omitting a commandment to love the world as such, John constructs a narrative world that invites critical reflection as well as affirmation on the part of the reader.

F. The Life of Prayer

To express the idea of praying, John uses both *aiteō* and *erōtaō*. The verb *aiteo* means "to ask for something, make a request." At one point John uses it in an everyday sense (4:9), but usually he employs it to express a request for spiritual gifts or gifts received in prayer (4:10; 11:22; 14:13, 14; 15:7, 16; 16:23, 24, 26). The verb *erōtaō* originally meant "to ask a question," and John often uses it with this meaning (1:19, 21, 25; 5:12; 9:2, 15, 19, 21, 23; 12:21; 16:5, 19, 30; 18:19, 21; 19:31, 38). In later Greek, *erōtaō* could also mean "to ask for something," and John uses it a number of times in this sense (4:31, 40, 47; 14:16; 16:26; 17:9, 15, 20; perhaps also 16:23). Usually the distinction is clear between the two meanings of *erōtaō*. In the sense of asking for something, *erōtaō* becomes a synonym of *aiteo*, and the two verbs together illustrate John's familiar tendency to use synonyms. John, as it happens, does not use other verbs to refer to the act of praying, such as *deomai* ("ask, beg"), *paraiteomai* ("ask, request"), *parakaleō* ("request, implore"), *proseuchomai* ("pray").

In arranging his gospel, John places most of his references to prayer within the Farewell Discourses (chs. 14-16), in which Jesus is preparing the disciples for his own departure and giving them instructions for their continuing existence in the post-resurrection period. In this way John indicates that his references to prayer are intended to have validity for the ongoing life of the early Christian community. The teachings that Jesus gave and the example that he set become normative for the church of later generations, as well as for the disciples during Jesus' earthly ministry.

In terms of relation analysis, it is significant that John speaks of prayer with regard to three distinct relationships, or three subject-object polarities. The disciples pray to Jesus (14:13, 14; probably 15:7). The disciples pray to God (15:16; 16:23, 26; probably 16:24). Jesus, as Son, also prays to God as Father (11:22; 14:16; 17:9, 15, 20). In addition, John evidently uses the Samaritan woman as a foil to illustrate potential discipleship: if she had known who Jesus was, she would have asked him and he would have given her "living water" (4:10). In this sense the Samaritan woman illustrates the type of relationship in which the disciples themselves are invited to pray to Jesus. It is probably accidental that John uses the verb *aiteō* for the first two relationships (in which the disciples are the subjects who pray), while he usually uses *erōtaō* for the third relationship (in which Jesus is the one who prays). The use of *aiteō* in 11:22 to describe Jesus' own petition to God suggests that John did think of these two verbs as synonyms.

Relation analysis serves not only to identify the three distinct relationships concerning which John speaks of asking or praying. Even more significantly, it helps to illustrate how John gives specific structure to relationships and correlates them with one another. When the disciples pray to Jesus, they are to ask in his "name" -- i.e., with reference to the totality of his person and work as the Son sent from the Father (14:13, 14). In a similar way, their "abiding" in Jesus and their obedience to his teachings establish the context for the petitions that they bring. In a highly poetic style of prose, John writes,

> If you abide in me,
>> and my words abide in you,
> ask whatever you will,
>> and it shall be done for you. (15:7)

In this way, John suggests, theological perception and obedient discipleship establish the contours of the relationship within which the disciples can pray for "whatever they will." They can pray for anything that is consonant with a true understanding of the person and work of Jesus himself, and consistent with their own commitment to obedience. Within this relationship, John indicates, the disciples have Jesus' promise that their prayers will be answered.

John indicates also that the relation of the disciples to Jesus informs their relation to God the Father, so that they are enabled to bring their petitions to the Father. When the disciples pray to the Father, they are to pray in the name of Jesus (15:16; 16:24, 26) or ask that the Father will grant their requests in the name of Jesus (16:23). It is significant that John never speaks simply of people praying directly to God. He always indicates that believers are to pray with reference to the "name" of Jesus. Their faith in Jesus as the Son and their relationship to him give structure to their relationship with God and establish the context in which they can bring their requests to God.

Jesus' own relationship to God means that his prayers to the Father can be simply and direct in a way that the disciples' prayers could not be. As the only Son (*huios*), Jesus enjoys a unique immediacy of relationship to the Father, in contrast to the derivative or mediate relation that believers have as "children" (*tekna*) of God. Thus Jesus can pray to God directly, whereas the disciples pray to God in the name of Jesus. Martha, for example, is sure that whatever Jesus asks from God, God will give him (11:22). In a similar way, Jesus assures the disciples that he will ask the Father, and the Father will give them another Advocate (14:16). John suggests, indeed, that Jesus' relation to the Father is so real and immediate that a specific petition, in the strict sense, would not be necessary; Jesus knows that the Father always hears him (11:41-42).

If Jesus' prayers to the Father can be simple and direct, they can also be complex in the sense that they reflect the relationships that Jesus and God have to believers. In presenting these prayers John makes a special effort, first of all, to avoid a misunderstanding which may have already risen in some circles of the church in his day. He does not want his readers to think of Jesus as the merciful Son interceding on behalf of believers to avert the wrath of an angry and vindictive God. It is not necessary for Jesus to intercede in this way because God already has love for Christian believers: the Father himself, Jesus assures his followers, already loves them (16:26-27). On the basis of God's love for believers, Jesus can then express his own concerns for them, asking on their behalf that God will protect them, sanctify them in the truth, and give them unity and love (17:6-26). In this way Jesus voluntarily modifies his prayer to God, so that it involves not only his own immediate relationship to God but also God's love for believers and his concern for their well-being in the world.

It is uncertain to what extent John thinks of Jesus' prayer in Chapter 17 as a model for all Christians to follow. Jesus, on the one hand, is the only Son of God, and his prayer will reflect his unique relationship to the Father as well as the circumstances that affect him directly at this point. It is very possible, on the other hand, that John also presents this prayer as a model that Christian believers can follow in ways that are appropriate for them. In this sense it is especially significant that the prayer is multi-relational. Jesus does not simply limit his words to his own relation to the Father, but he voluntarily refers to the Father's relationship of love to believers, and then with reference to this he gives expression, through intercession, to his own relation to them. In this way John may well be suggesting that true Christian prayer, like Jesus' own prayer, always takes into account the complex of interacting relationships in which the community of believers finds its *raison d'être*.

In another respect too John may be thinking of Jesus' prayer as a model for Christians to follow. A very difficult problem with regard to intercessory prayer is that it may seem to be unnecessary. If God already loves people and knows their needs, he should, it would seem, take care of their needs directly without waiting for other people to intercede for them. Perhaps John had already encountered this problem in his own time and wishes to address it at this point. It is significant, at any rate, that John seems to present Jesus as offering the prototype of superfluous intercessory prayer. Because the Father already loves believers, he would presumably be concerned to meet their needs even without the Son's intervention on their behalf. The Son, nevertheless, offers precisely the intercession that may seem so unnecessary. At this point too, John seems to indicate, Christians need to follow the example that Jesus has given.

Although it does not offer a simple solution to the problem of intercessory prayer, relation analysis does help to clarify the dynamics of the process by pointing out how one relationship can enrich another. Jesus can presuppose God's relationship of love to believers (16:26-27). He knows also that God has given to him those believers whom he loves (17:9-10). Rather than let God's love operate independently, as it were, Jesus himself offers intercession on behalf of believers, including those of later generations (17:9, 20). In praying on their behalf, he knows that he is praying for those whom God already loves, but he still prays on their behalf. In this way he incorporates God's relationship to believers into his own relationship to them.

Jesus' words mean that a new situation arises, a *novum*, in which believers receive not only God's love but also Jesus' prayers on their behalf -- prayers which presuppose and express God's love. Perhaps John would say that God's love becomes more concretely effective in this way. John does, at any rate, depict Jesus engaging in intercessory prayer, incorporating God's relation to believers into his own relation to them. John also seems to suggest that Jesus becomes an example at this point as believers offer their own intercessory prayers on behalf of others. Believers, too, can incorporate God's love for people into their own prayers for them, allowing one relationship to enhance and enrich another.

This kind of analysis suggests, paradoxically, that God's love for believers is all-sufficient and yet in a sense incomplete. The Father's love for believers must be all-sufficient because it comes from the Father; love from this source could not be less than perfect. Yet the Father's love is incomplete in the sense that it does not, in itself, include the Son's love for believers. The Father's love becomes effectively complete when the Son voluntarily appropriates it and incorporates it into his own relationship to believers. When John depicts Jesus at prayer in Chapter 17, he presents a paradigm for the type of prayer in which one relationship becomes complete when it is allowed to inform and enrich another. Perhaps in this way John wishes to provide a theological rationale for the intercessory prayer that Christians offer on behalf of others: although God's love is all-sufficient in itself, it can become effectively complete only when believers voluntarily make it a part of their own relationship to others.

In this way the phenomenon of intercessory prayer illustrates John's general view that prayer is multi-relational, involving more than two parties and more than one relationship. Believers, for example, do not simply pray to God or Jesus. They pray to the Father in the name of Jesus (15:16; 16:24, 26), or they ask the Father to grant their prayer in the name of Jesus (16:23). They pray to Jesus in Jesus' own name, so that the Father may be glorified in the Son (14:13-14), or they pray to Jesus as the vine in whom they abide and whose vinegrower is the Father (15:1, 7). Even when Jesus prays, he does not simply pray for people; he prays on their behalf (17:6-26), knowing that the Father already loves them (16:26-27). Christian prayer, John suggests, occurs within the context of these relationships involving the Father, the Son, and believers. As Christian prayer, it could not occur apart from these relationships. Because it does occur within them, prayer becomes richer and more meaningful than it would be otherwise.

The fact that John thinks of prayer as multi-relational may explain, in part, why he often refrains from giving it specific content. In many instances Jesus assures his followers that they will receive "anything" or "whatever" they ask (14:13-14; 15:7, 16; 16:23), as if there were no limits at all to the content of their petitions. Jesus also makes it clear, however, that believers are to ask in his name -- i.e., in a way that is consonant with their relationship to him and their total understanding of his person and work (14:13-14; 15:16; 16:24, 26). In a similar way, the disciples, by "abiding" in Jesus, receive a relationship to him that establishes the conditions and the context for the prayers that they offer (15:7). Whether they are praying to Jesus or the Father, the disciples, John suggests, would not think of asking for anything that is inconsistent with the "name" of Jesus or their "abiding" in him. If John does not define appropriate prayer by specifying its content, he does so by delineating the relationships within which it occurs.

When John does refer to the content of prayer, it is significant that he focuses on the concept of eternal life as a present reality for Christian believers. Those who know who Jesus truly is can ask him for the gift of "living water" (4:10), which will well up within them to "eternal life" (4:14). Jesus himself, according to Martha, can ask whatever he wishes from the Father (11:22), but Martha here is clearly hoping for the gift of new life for her brother, Lazarus. This life, in turn, is a symbol for the eternal life that Jesus offers to all believers (11:23-27). Whether believers are praying or Jesus himself is praying, the object of petition is the gift of eternal life.

Through this focus on eternal life, John suggests that the gifts of prayer are gifts of the new age. Eternal life, a feature of the age to come, is already a present reality for Christian believers (e.g., 3:36; 5:24). In other references to prayer, John also indicates that he perceives it within the context of the new age. In their ongoing life as a Christian community, believers will pray "in that day" (16:23-26) -- an expression that suggests the age to come but refers now, for John, to the post-resurrection period that has already arrived. In a similar way John assures believers that their prayers will be answered so that their "joy" may be complete (16:24; cf. 17:13). Through prayer, the joyfulness of the new age becomes a present reality of Christian experience. Although John recognizes that Christians still live in a hostile world, he views prayer as a point -- perhaps the central point -- at which the reality of the new age is given and received.

This emphasis on eternal life indicates that, just as John thinks of the process of prayer in terms of relationships, he also thinks of the object of prayer in the same way. Christians pray especially for the gift of eternal life. This means, according to the only passage in which John defines the term, that they may "know" the only true God and Jesus Christ whom he has sent (17:3). In using the word "know," John employs an Old Testament idea signifying faithful and obedient covenant relationship. Ancient Israel, for example, was called to show "knowledge of God" by being faithful to her covenant with Yahweh and fulfilling her ethical obligations under this covenant (Hos. 4:1-3).

In a similar way, "knowing," for John, is primarily a term of relationship. To "know" God and Christ is to stand in the right relationship with them as they have made themselves known and issue their call to discipleship. Since these are life-giving relationships, they constitute the essence of eternal life, and eternal life in turn can be defined in terms of relationship. For John, the process of prayer involves relationships, in the sense that Christians pray for one another and pray to God or Jesus in the name of Jesus. At the same time, the object of prayer is also defined in terms of relationship, in the sense that Christians pray for the eternal life that consists in "knowing" God and Jesus. From the standpoint of relation analysis, the process of prayer already anticipates the object that it seeks.

As an author addressing a reader -- the implied reader whose role may be accepted by the actual reader -- John constructs a narrative world in which the topic of prayer is much more complex than the actual reader might at first assume. In a significant omission, John refrains from saying that people simply pray directly to God or to Jesus. He emphasizes instead the network of relationships involving the Father, the Son, and believers as the essential framework in which prayer takes place. In a similar way, with regard to intercessory prayer especially, John emphasizes that one relationship can appropriate and incorporate another, as when Jesus incorporates the Father's love for believers into his own prayer on their behalf. John uses the device of paradox in depicting God's love as all-sufficient in itself yet brought to concrete actuality through intercessory prayer. When he speaks of eternal life as the object of prayer, John uses the technique of paradox once more by indicating that the process of prayer anticipates its content, since the process and the content both focus on relationships involving God and persons. In all these ways John alerts the reader to differences between the narrative world of the gospel and the everyday world of human experience. In all these ways too he challenges the reader to perceive how the relational context brings a fresh perspective to the topic of prayer.

CHAPTER IV

Believers and the World: The Mission of Faith

A. The "World"

The relationship between believers and the world provides the possibility and establishes the necessity for the mission of faith. It also functions to shape the strategy of mission and sustain the hope that mission will achieve its goals, even on those occasions when it appears to fail. Without some form of positive relationship, believers and the world would remain separate, each existing as a self-contained entity apart from the other. Whether they would simply ignore one another or actually come into conflict, the concept of the mission of faith would be absent.

The purpose of the present chapter is to analyze John's understanding of the relationship between believers and the world. As it was suggested in the Preface, each chapter of this study, in general, presupposes those that precede. "Believers," in this sense, can be understood as those who find the source of faith, the actuality of faith, and the community of faith in the relationships that have been delineated in the first three chapters. At this point it is appropriate to examine John's view of the "world" and then analyze his understanding of the relationship between believers and the world as the basis for mission to the world.

John evidently takes very seriously the term "world" (*kosmos*), since he uses it so often and in so many settings throughout his gospel. He uses the word some 78 times, more often than any other New Testament writer, employing it in a wide variety of settings in almost every chapter of his gospel. Through this usage John may well be suggesting an important, if preliminary, point -- Jesus did not live in a cultural and spiritual vacuum, any more than believers could live in such a vacuum. Each had to live in the world and enter into some form of engagement with the world as the context for a life of faith and obedience.

In a number of passages John uses the term "world" in a way that could refer to the created, material world.[24] In speaking of the Word, for example, John states that "the world came into being through him" (1:10), and elsewhere he refers to the glory of the Son "before the world existed" (17:5) or "before the foundation of the world" (17:24). In passages such as these John is thinking primarily of the created world of nature, the material world with its many kinds of living beings, that was created "through" the Word of God. In contrast to gnostic thought, John may also be emphasizing the intrinsic goodness of the material world, since a world created through the Word could not be other than good (1:10; cf. 1:3).

John also uses the term "world" to depict the realm of human life, as it is organized into its own social structures, formulates its own values and priorities, and pursues its own ends. Most, if not all, of the passages in which John speaks of the material world could also refer to the world of human society. When John says that the Word, for example, "was in the world" (1:10), he could understand the term in both senses, and very possibly he could be expecting his readers to understand it in both senses -- the Word lived a human life in the created world, and at the same time the Word encountered the attitudes, values, and institutions of human society. In this respect John's use of "world" illustrates his stylistic trait of using words or phrases with a double meaning.

In many other passages as well, John also uses "world" to designate some aspect of human society or human life. In these passages the sense of "created world" has receded into the background, and it becomes clear that John is especially interested in exploring the relationship between divine reality and human life. When John writes of the Word, for example, that "the world did not know him" (1:10), John is clearly thinking of the reaction of humanity to the Word. Whether a particular passage can refer to the created world as well as human society, or whether it simply refers to human society, it is important to investigate John's understanding of "world" as the self-contained sphere of human life, with its values, priorities, and social structures.

When he speaks of the "world" of human life, John seems to be thinking of it in three ways: it is the world as the object of God's action, it is the world as the subject of its own acting, and it is the world as the subject of God's hope. Although, in theory, some of these meanings could overlap, it usually seems in any particular instance that John is looking at the "world" primarily from one of these points of view.

As the object of God's action, the world is the realm into which light has come (1:9; 3:19), i.e., the realm in which Christ has appeared as the light of the world (8:12; 9:5; 12:46). It is the world that God loved so fully that he gave his only Son, that believers might have everlasting life (3:16). In a very similar way, it is the world to which God sent his Son, or to which the Son has come (3:17; 10:36; 11:27; 12:46; 16:28; 17:18; 18:37). The world is the object of God's purpose of salvation, given expression through the Son (3:17; 4:42; 12:47). The world receives, or is intended to receive, life from the Son (6:33, 51), and in a similar way it can receive from the Son what the Son has heard from the Father (8:26).

In all these ways John indicates how deeply God cares for the world, how actively God has expressed his love for the world, and how strongly God seeks the salvation of the world. God has, John implies, done everything possible for humanity, even to the point of sending his own Son into the world. As Christian believers, in turn, address the world, they must recognize that their relationship to the world always has its basis in God's own attitude and action toward the world. Whether they find the world receptive, indifferent, or hostile, they must always seek to perceive it as the world that God loved and the world that God continues to love.

Just as John sees the world as the object of God's action, he also sees it, at the same time, as the subject of its own acting. He can perceive it one way in faith, and the other way through empirical observation. John finds it necessary to record, therefore that the world refuses to acknowledge either the Word (1:10) or the Father (17:25). It hates the Son (7:7; 15:18), and it hates the disciples (15:18, 19; 17:14). The world has sin (1:29; 16:8-9), and it is liable to judgment (9:39; 12:31). As John perceives it most often, the world seems to be a self-contained sphere of human life, adhering to its own values and priorities.[25] In this sense it is governed by its own principles and power structures, or its own "ruler" (*archōn*: 12:31; 14:30; 16:11).

In describing the world as the subject of its own acting, John is seeking to record his observations as accurately as possible. He is undoubtedly expressing his understanding of the world's response to Jesus, beginning from the time of Jesus' earthly ministry and continuing up to his own day. John knows that "humanity" or people in general have often denied Jesus and rejected Christian faith, and he seems to grieve that the world has so often acted as it has. In this respect he views the life of the world as a tragic failure to respond to God's love made known in Christ. This is the context in which John notes that Jesus does not pray for the world (17:9). To do so, as Barrett remarks, would be "almost an absurdity," because the "only hope" for the world "is precisely that it should cease to be" the world.[26]

At the same time, John recognizes that some people have responded positively to Jesus. He knows that some believed in him and became "children of God" (1:12), in consonance with God's own purpose (1:13). In this respect, at least, the world can not simply be identified with humanity in general. It is also significant that John never speaks of the "world" as inherently evil. It does, indeed, have "sin," and it is subject to the dominance of its own power structures. John seems to believe, however, that the world of humanity, like the material world, was created through the Word of God and must therefore be intrinsically or potentially good. No matter how much sin the world has accumulated through its own lack of belief, John wants to perceive the world of humanity, as well as the material world, as God's creation.

John sees the world as the object of God's action and as the subject of its own acting. The first perspective always remains primary, but it engages in continual dialogue, as it were, with the second. The world as the object of God's action is also the world that acts through its own responses of belief or unbelief. On the basis of this continual dialogue between the two perspectives, John can also perceive the world in a third way, as the subject of God's hope. The world, for example, was made through the Word of God (1:10); thus the world was intended for faith in the Word, and faith, in this sense, should be "natural" for those in the world. God loved the world (3:16) and sent his Son into the world with the purpose "that the world might be saved through him" (3:17). In this respect salvation itself should be "natural" for the world, resulting logically from God's intention. Toward the close of his life, Jesus insists that he and his disciples are not of the world (17:14, 16). Yet Jesus does not want the disciples to retreat into a private type of pietism. He sends them into the world, that the world may know that the Father has sent him and has loved the disciples (17:18, 21, 23). In ways such as these John expresses his belief that the world, in spite of all its sin, remains the subject of God's hope.

The method of relation analysis suggests that the relationship between believers and the world may be correlated with these three ways of understanding the "world." In faith, believers see the world as the object of God's action -- the world that God created, loves, and wishes to save. In this respect believers stand in a positive relationship to the world, appreciating it and supporting it whenever it reflects God's purposes. Through empirical analysis, believers also perceive the world as the subject of its own acting, often following its own ways of unbelief and pursuing its own ends. Although believers do not sever their relationship with the world at this point, they recognize that they are engaged with it in its actuality and its opposition to God's purposes. In hope, finally, believers see the world as the subject of God's own hope. They remain active in the world, knowing that they are sent into the world by the Son just as the Son was sent by the Father. Their understanding of the future is open-ended because they continually seek to share the hope that God sustains toward the world. Correlating with one another these three ways of understanding the world, believers define their relationship to the world and engage in mission to the world.

As John constructs his narrative world for the reader, he wants the reader to be aware of these aspects of the "world" of human society, which always has its own values and priorities. To actualize the text, John implies, is to become a Christian believer, and to become a believer is to enter into multi-relational engagement with the world. The believer can not retreat from the world or adopt any simplistic stance toward it. The believer, John stresses, must always be able to see the world as the object of God's action, the subject of its own action, and the continuing subject of God's hope. As a technique for addressing the reader and stimulating the reader to adopt a multi-relational perspective on the world, John emphasizes in this way the significant difference between his narrative world and the attitudes or expectations that the reader may have already developed.

B. John the Baptist

The method of relation analysis also helps the reader of John's gospel to perceive that the relation between John the Baptist and the world is parallel to that between believers and the world. John the Baptist relates to the world by bringing it his testimony concerning Jesus. In a similar way, believers bring their testimony to the world, bearing witness to Jesus as their Lord. In this respect John the Baptist becomes a prototype of the church in its mission to the world.

When he first introduces the Baptist, John describes four salient characteristics of his work: he was sent from God, he came to bear testimony to the light, he did so that all might believe, and he indicated clearly that he himself was not the light (1:6-8). John's further description of the Baptist's activities gives an explication of these four main features of his work. The Baptist, for example, prepares the way for Jesus, baptizes as testimony to Jesus, proclaims Jesus as the Lamb of God who takes away sin, testifies that the Spirit abides on Jesus, proclaims Jesus as the Son of God, and voluntarily gives up his disciples to Jesus (1:19-40). Finally, in a summary that probably represents his last words in the gospel, the Baptist declares that he is willing to "decrease" that Jesus may "increase" (3:30).

The fact that the Baptist allows two of his disciples to follow Jesus (1:35-40) may well be John's way of establishing a connection between the Baptist's activity and Jesus' ministry. From one point of view, this incident can emphasize Jesus' independence. It stresses, that is, that Jesus felt free to begin his own ministry while the Baptist was still active, even attracting some of the Baptist's disciples into his own movement.

From the standpoint of relation analysis, this incident can also point to the correspondence between the Baptist's ministry and Jesus' own ministry. As the Baptist relates to the world by bringing testimony concerning Jesus, so he transmit this function to the followers of Jesus, who represent in this respect the beginnings of the church. In this way the relationship between the Baptist and the world serves as a model for the relationship between Christian believers and the world as they, in turn, bring their own testimony concerning Jesus.

For this reason the four characteristics of the Baptist's work that John delineates in 1:6-8 become especially important as a paradigm for the relationship of believers to the world. As John the Baptist was sent from God (1:6), so believers should be sent from God. Their witness to the world is authentic only to the extent that they represent God's presence and seek to implement his will for human life. The sense of being sent from God becomes a criterion by which believers should always test the validity of their own motives and activities. Only by continually examining their work in light of this criterion can they engage in mission to the world.

In a similar way, as the Baptist came to bear testimony to Jesus (1:7), believers understand their own work in terms of bringing this witness to the world. Some will do this directly, and others indirectly. They may bring the "good news" of Jesus Christ through preaching and teaching, or they may work in other ways to be of service to people in the world. In either case they understand their relationship to the world in terms of bearing witness to Jesus and pointing to his significance for human life. Although they may seek in many different ways to enhance the quality of human life, they see their activities, from the standpoint of faith, as ways of bearing witness to Jesus Christ.

As a third aspect of his work, John the Baptist bore witness "so that all might believe through him" (1:7). The word translated "so that" (*hina*) probably expresses here both the purpose and the intended result of the Baptist's work. The Baptist himself did not actually attain this goal. Whether or not believers can ever achieve it, they inherit this purpose and seek this result in fulfilling their own mission in the world. There is, John suggests, a certain open-endedness about the work of the church in the world, but he would always want the church to have this purpose and hope for this result.

As a fourth characteristic of the Baptist's work, John indicates that the Baptist made no claim himself to be the light to which he was testifying (1:8). From one point of view, this statement emphasizes the distinction between the Baptist and Jesus -- the Baptist is not the Christ; Jesus alone is the Christ. From the standpoint of relation analysis, this statement points to a correlation of relationships that is central for John's understanding of the church and Christian discipleship. Just as the Baptist related to the world without making claims for himself, so Christian believers are to relate to the world without concern for their own status or interests. Only in this way, John suggests, can they continue to nurture the relationship with the world that John the Baptist initiated.

As a strategy for addressing the reader, John develops the analogy between the role of the Baptist and the role that the reader would assume by entering into engagement with the text. As the Baptist acted in the world, so the reader would be expected to act as a result of actualizing the text. John's analogy ties together the narrative world of the text and the empirical world in which the reader would be active. John probably expects that the reader will find the narrative world different in some ways, and similar in others, to the familiar everyday world. In either case, John indicates, the reader knows what would be involved in a response to the text, and the reader can consider what decision to make. In this respect John's use of analogy helps the reader to perceive in advance the consequences of actualizing the text.

C. Nicodemus

Jesus' discussion with Nicodemus (3:1-21) illustrates another dimension of the relationship between believers and the world. Whereas John the Baptist served as a model for believers themselves in bringing testimony to the world, Nicodemus illustrates several aspects of the world to which Christians bring their message. Nicodemus represents most immediately the Jewish world that is sympathetic to Jesus and has formed a limited understanding of his role. More generally, Nicodemus symbolizes all those in the world of human society who are interested in learning about Jesus and have possibly arrived at a preliminary stage of belief in him. The discussion with Nicodemus is important, finally, because it highlights the role of the Spirit in facilitating the relationship between Christians and the world.

When he first comes to Jesus, Nicodemus already regards him as "a teacher who has come from God" (3:2). Nicodemus also believes that the signs which Jesus does confirm him in this role (3:2). Nicodemus' view of Jesus is unusually positive for a Pharisee, since, at least in the synoptic gospels, the Pharisees were usually very critical of Jesus. In reply to Nicodemus, however, Jesus emphasizes the need for him to be born *anōthen* -- that is, born "anew" through the means of the Spirit that comes "from above" (3:3, 7). John is suggesting in this way that it is not sufficient, for Jews or for people generally, to think of Jesus simply as a teacher, even one who comes from God and performs signs. Beyond this, as John indicates later in the passage, people must be able to perceive Jesus as the Son of man (3:13-14), the Son (3:16-17), and the Son of God (3:18). The impressive accumulation of titles emphasizes the contrast between acceptance of Jesus simply as a teacher and belief in him in his relation of sonship to the Father.

John mentions the Spirit three times in this passage, each time in connection with the idea of being "born" (3:5, 6, 8). In this way John wishes to indicate that the Spirit has a vital role in effecting the transition that Nicodemus must make from unbelief or limited faith to a full faith in Jesus. The Spirit here has an enabling function in making it possible for Nicodemus to be "born anew," acquiring a complete faith in Jesus and entering the new life that is now available to him. Although John seems to think of faith primarily in terms of believing in Jesus as Christ or Son of God, he also recognizes that faith involves an understanding of conceptual beliefs. In the remainder of the passage, therefore, he speaks of the meaning of topics such as resurrection, life, salvation, and judgment (3:11-21).

The changes from singular "you" to plural "you" in the passage (3:7, 11, 12) suggest that John is thinking on two levels at once: Jesus is addressing Nicodemus, about the year A.D. 30; and the early Christian community, around the end of the first century, is addressing those who have no faith or only a partial faith. In this latter sense the passage depicts with special clarity the relationship between believers and the world. The Spirit has an integral role in this relationship. Rather surprisingly, he does not serve at this point to inspire and empower the disciples of Jesus as they bring the gospel to the world. The Spirit functions instead to help persons in the world make the critical transition to the new life of faith. In this way the Spirit facilitates the missionary work of the disciples by helping those in the world achieve the transformation of values and beliefs involved in the process or event of being "born anew."

When John was describing the work of the Baptist, he outlined the relation to the world that the reader would assume as a result of actualizing the text of the gospel. Now, when John speaks of Nicodemus, he presents the complementary thought that the Spirit of God will assist the reader in carrying out this role, since it is the function of the Spirit at this point to help unbelievers turn to faith. John, in effect, assures the reader of the Spirit's help if the reader continues the work of the Baptist and bears testimony to the world. Indirectly, too, John also assures the reader of the Spirit's help as the reader makes his or her own transition from unbelief to belief. In this way John reflects his understanding that actualizing the text may involve more than one process for the reader and more than one role for the Spirit.

D. Judea: Patterns of Response

The methodology of relation analysis suggests that Jesus' visit to Judea in 7:1-52 may serve as a model for the patterns of positive or negative response that the disciples themselves will encounter in their mission to the world. Just as Jesus brought his message to Judea, so the disciples will bring their message to the world. Just as Jesus encountered "division" (*schisma*, 7:43) as a result of his ministry in Judea, so the disciples will meet different kinds of response when they bring their witness to the world. Just as Jesus was ultimately "successful" in Judea, in spite of apparent failure, so the disciples will be "successful" because of the intrinsic integrity of their ministry in the world.

In depicting Jesus' visit to Judea, John suggests first that Judea can represent the "world" generally as the sphere of human life and culture, with its own values and priorities. To present this symbolism he arranges his description according to a pattern of A, B, A', B'. He indicates first that Judea is the place of danger, where the Jews were seeking to kill Jesus (7:1). Judea, nevertheless, is the place where Jesus must go to manifest himself and his works (7:3-4). John then changes his terminology from "Judea" to the "world": the world hates Jesus because he testifies that its works are evil (7:7). When Jesus finally goes to Judea, he meets different responses, as people react to him positively or negatively (7:12). Thus Judea, the place of danger (A), is the place where Jesus must go (B); Judea represents the world generally (A'), where Jesus receives different responses to his activity (B').

By treating Judea as representative of the world generally, John indicates that Jesus' visit to Judea can serve as a paradigm for the work of the disciples as they too bring their message to the world. The world is a place of danger for the disciples, as it was for Jesus (A); the disciples too face persecution or even death (cf. 15:18-16:4). Yet the world, at the same time, is the place where the disciples must go (B); they can not retreat from the world, any more than Jesus himself did so. As Jesus perceived the hostility of the world and yet brought his message to the world, so must the disciples face the dangers of the world and yet testify to it.

Even if they are hated by the world, the disciples must continue Jesus' testimony that the works of the world are evil (A'); it belongs to the integrity of their mission to differentiate between their message to the world and the values and priorities of the world itself. Just as Jesus received different responses to his work, so the disciples must anticipate a varied pattern of responses, positive or negative, that people will make to their testimony (B'); they must expect these reactions and be prepared to deal with them as constructively as possible. In all these ways, John indicates that the followers of Jesus can learn and benefit from Jesus' own example in engagement with the world.

In the remainder of the chapter (7:14-52), John develops the theme that Jesus received differing reactions to his testimony in Judea. John arranges these reactions as a pattern of alternating negative and positive responses. Negatively, people are skeptical of Jesus on the grounds that no one will know where the Messiah comes from (7:27). Positively, people think that Jesus' signs are indeed those of the Messiah (7:31). Negatively, people do not understand where Jesus intends to go (7:33-36). Positively, some people believe in Jesus as Messiah because of his words about the Spirit (7:37-41a). Negatively, other people object that the Messiah can not come from Galilee (7:41b-42). Positively, the officers sent to arrest Jesus are impressed by his teachings (7:45-46). Negatively, the authorities and the Pharisees reject Jesus (7:48). Positively, Nicodemus pleads for a fair hearing for Jesus (7:50-51). Negatively, the Pharisees object that no prophet is to come from Galilee (7:52).

In this list of alternating reactions to Jesus, John seems to reflect his own conviction that people were accepting Jesus for the right reasons and rejecting him for the wrong reasons. It is very important, for example, to respond to Jesus as Messiah in word and deed, and to understand him fairly on his own terms; it is, in the final analysis, unimportant whether or not Jesus came from Galilee. In this sense John wishes to indicate not only that Jesus met different responses in Judea, but also that the responses themselves reflect differing levels of spiritual understanding.

John wishes to indicate further that believers too, as they interact with the world, are constantly engaged with alternating patterns of response from the world. Sometimes these responses are positive; sometimes they are negative. Just as Jesus himself encountered both kinds of response, John suggests that believers will do so. It is part of their work to meet both kinds of reaction. Yet it is also part of their faith that they will ultimately be "successful" in bringing their message to the world, just as Jesus himself was ultimately "successful" in accomplishing his work. The criterion of success, however, is authenticity of word and deed rather than immediately apparent and quantifiable results. Jesus was successful in the sense that he brought a true message of everlasting life from God the Father. In a similar way, the disciples will be successful by bearing genuine testimony to Jesus, even if, as John implies, they continually encounter patterns of alternating response from the world.

In this way, paradoxically, John combines an open-endedness about the future with a firm assurance of success. His view of the future is open-ended because he does not indicate, and probably does not assume that he knows, whether positive responses will outnumber negative ones or *vice versa*. John is certain that believers will indeed encounter both kinds of response as they work in the world; he seems much less certain which kind of response, in terms of measurable results, will prevail over the other.

John's main interest lies in the authenticity of the believers' work in the world. He measures success, not by quantifiable results, but by the integrity of the testimony that believers bear in their engagement with the world. Here and now, believers can be successful if they bring an authentic witness of word and deed to the world, just as Jesus himself was successful by virtue of the integrity of the testimony that he bore. In this respect John can think of success as a present, ongoing reality, much as he thinks of eternal life itself as a present reality for the believer.

In his account of Jesus' words to Nicodemus, John assured the reader of the help of the Spirit as the reader turned from unbelief to belief and then assumed the work of helping others make the same transition. At this point John adds the further thought that bearing testimony to Jesus has value in itself and is "successful" in itself, even if this testimony meets with a mixed set of responses. In doing this work, the reader would be following in the direction marked out by Jesus himself and taken up by his disciples. John places these themes into his narrative world so that the reader will understand, as fully as possible, what actualization of the text would entail.

E. Judea: Patterns of Interaction

The setting for Chapter 9, in which Jesus heals the man born blind, is the same as that for Chapters 7 and 8. Jesus is still in Jerusalem at the festival of Tabernacles, and he is still presented as "the light of the world" (9:5). In Chapter 9, however, John develops the theme of light in a different way, connecting it with the idea of seeing as a human capacity, and then using physical sight as a symbol for spiritual perception or insight. In this sense John uses the events of Chapter 9 to illustrate the importance of spiritual perception as a component of faith. The man who was born blind receives spiritual sight as well as physical sight, as he gradually passes from ignorance about Jesus (9:12) to faith in him as a prophet (9:17) and a man from God (9:33), and then finally he worships Jesus as Son of man and Lord (9:35-38). The Pharisees, conversely, think that they see very well, but they are shown to be spiritually blind because they can not perceive who Jesus really is (9:39-41). This contrast between spiritual sight and spiritual blindness is one of the major components of the narrative world that John wishes to bring to the attention of the reader.

John also uses the narrative in Chapter 9 to treat other important aspects of Christian faith, although he does not always develop these fully. He refers, for example, to the popular belief of the time that illness or disability is punishment for sin, indicating that this belief was reflected by the disciples (9:2), maintained by the Pharisees (9:34), but rejected by Jesus (9:3). At several points John alludes to the question, which was evidently widespread among the Jews, whether or not Jesus was a genuine emissary from God (9:16, 24, 29, 31, 33). As John relates his story, he indicates that Christian faith must see Jesus not simply as rabbi (9:2) or prophet (9:17), or even as Messiah (9:22), but ultimately as Son of man (9:35-37) and Lord (9:36-38). John employs this narrative, finally, to present his characteristic understanding of "judgment" (krima, 9:39) as division or separation between those who have faith in Jesus and those who do not. In this respect judgment is a continuing process that people sustain themselves as they respond positively or negatively to Jesus and his mission.[27]

From the standpoint of relation analysis, John employs the narrative of Chapter 9 to introduce the reader to a "world" in which Jesus' actions have both direct and indirect effects. In this case the direct consequence of healing the blind man was that the man gradually came to "see" Jesus and acquire faith in him (9:35-39). The indirect effect of Jesus' action was that other groups of people reacted in various ways to the blind man and to one another. To illustrate this "ripple effect" of the healing, John presents a series of interrogations or miniature trials in which these secondary groups interact with the man or with each other: neighbors and acquaintances question the man (9:8-12), the Pharisees examine the man (9:15-17), the

"Jews" (evidently used here as equivalent to the Pharisees; cf. 9:24, 27) interrogate the man's parents (9:18-23), the Jews examine the man himself (9:24-34), and finally Jesus questions the man (9:35-38).

Of these five scenes, the first four all involve persons or groups in the world as they interact with someone directly affected by Jesus' actions or with one another. These groups reflect different attitudes, such as curiosity (9:8-12), fear (9:18-23), and hostility (9:15-17, 23-34), although it is doubtful whether John wishes to describe a full range of possible reactions. These interrogation scenes are all inconclusive, since John is more interested in pointing to the need for faith in Jesus than in offering "proof" of his significance. John's main purpose in presenting these miniature trials is to emphasize that Jesus' actions have not only direct consequences but also indirect effects which can be important in their own right. In this way John alerts his readers to the importance of identifying and understanding the indirect consequences of Jesus' actions, as secondary groups of people, in their own ways and from their own perspectives, respond to the revelation that Jesus has brought.

When believers bring their message to the world, they will encounter the same kind of situation that Jesus himself found. Their message will have an immediate effect, as it touches some persons directly, and it will also have indirect consequences as other people interact with those directly affected or with one another. Just as Jesus' actions in the world produced a multiplicity of effects and elicited a variety of responses from different groups of people, so the relation of the disciples to the world must be worked out in connection with a multiplicity of relationships existing within the world itself, as other religions or patterns of social and cultural values establish their competing claims on persons in the world.

In dealing with this complex of relationships, John suggests that believers must be guided by two principles, which he presents at the beginning and the end of the chapter -- the need to persist in doing the work of God as long as the opportunity is present (9:4-5), and the need to recognize the critical significance of believing in Jesus as the criterion that differentiates the life of the Christian from the life of those in the world (9:35-41). These two principles stand as pillars supporting the weight of the chapter. If disciples follow these, John implies, they can deal constructively with the direct effects of their work and the complex of interactions that will follow.

As he addresses the reader, in particular, John wants to provide several paradigms of ways in which people may respond to the work of Jesus. The man who was healed responded in one way. Neighbors and acquaintances, the Pharisees, and the man's parents responded in other ways. Although he does not approve of all these responses, John does want to indicate that a range of responses is possible. To help guide the reader in choosing among potential responses, John gives the example of the blind man himself, who understands very little at first but gradually arrives at more mature faith in Jesus.

F. Sending into the World

As part of the conversation at the Last Supper, John begins to develop the theme of "sending," with special reference to the correlation between the sending of the Son into the world and then the sending of the disciples into the world. On this occasion Jesus says to the disciples, "Very truly, I tell you, servants are not greater than their master, nor are messengers greater than the one who sent them" (13:16). For "messengers," John uses the word *apostolos*, literally "one who is sent," as a way of highlighting the relationship between the one who sends and the one who is sent.

Several verses later John explores more fully the range of relationships involved in this central theme of "sending." At this point Jesus remarks, "Very truly, I tell you, whoever receives one whom I send receives me; and whoever receives me receives him who sent me" (13:20). This verse in turn anticipates Jesus' reference to "sending" in his prayer to the Father: "As you have sent me into the world, so I have sent them into the world" (17:18). Finally Jesus, as risen Lord, commissions his disciples to go into the world: "As the Father has sent me, so I send you" (20:21). In these last three verses (13:20; 17:18; 20:21), John indicates clearly that he thinks of "sending" in terms of a correlation between the Father's action in sending the Son and the Son's action in sending the disciples.

In his account of the public ministry of Jesus -- i.e., in the first twelve chapters of the gospel, up to the Last Supper in Chapter 13 -- John has not emphasized Jesus' intention to send the disciples into the world. Although he has referred occasionally to the idea of sending, he has preferred to focus on other aspects of this theme. He has indicated, for example, that God sent the Baptist to bear testimony to Jesus (1:6, 33; 3:28), and he has often described Jesus as the Son who was sent by the Father. Indeed, John speaks of Jesus in this way in a wide variety of settings and in every chapter from 3 through 12, as well as in most of the following chapters. These descriptions of Jesus, as the Son sent from the Father, become a common thread that helps to bind together the diverse materials and settings in the narrative of his public ministry. A typical example occurs in the summary of Jesus' teaching that John gives at the close of the public ministry: "Then Jesus cried aloud: 'Whoever believes in me believes not in me but in him who sent me. And whoever sees me sees him who sent me'" (12: 44-45).

From the standpoint of relation analysis the concept of "sending" is especially important because it involves a complex of relationships which stand in close interrelation with one another. To say that the Father sends the Son into the world, for example, means that the Father has a relation to the Son, the Father has a relation to the world, and the Son acquires a new relation to the world. Because the Father has a relation to the Son, he can send the Son. The action of sending the Son into the world, further, means that the Father assumes a commitment toward the world that effectively strengthens his existing relation to the world as the Creator of the world. As a result of being sent into the world, the Son also enters into a new involvement with the world. The Father had a relation to the Son before he sent the Son, but his action of sending gave overt expression to this relation. In a similar way the Father had a relation to the world before he sent the Son, but his action of sending the Son both expressed and deepened his relation to the world. The Son, as the incarnate Word, also had a relation to the world before he was sent into the world, but this relation now assumed a deeper and more specific form. In each case some form of relationship preceded God's action of sending, but then this relationship was at least partially transformed by the action of sending itself.

A similar set of circumstances would characterize the action of the Son himself in sending the disciples into the world. Again, this would mean that the Son has a relation to the disciples, the Son has a relation to the world, and the disciples have a relation to the world. Each relationship existed in some significant way beforehand, and each relationship is at least partially transformed when the Son commissions the disciples to go into the world. The methodology of relation analysis seeks, as far as possible, to identify the contours of each relationship, and then it asks what meanings John is communicating by correlating these relationships with one another.

In the present context the analysis comes to a focus on the meaning of the terms "as... so" (*kathōs...kai*) in 17:18 and 20:21. In his prayer, for example, Jesus says to the Father, "As you have sent me into the world, so I have sent them into the world" (17:18). The use of these correlative words raises the question how the relationship of the Father to the world governs the relationship of the Son to the world, or how the Father's action of sending the Son underlies the Son's own action of sending the disciples. Does the action of "sending," for example, have the same purposes and results in each case? It is clear that the Father's action of sending will serve in some way as a paradigm for the Son's own action of sending. Since John writes that the Father first sent John the Baptist, and then his own Son, it will be appropriate to treat together these two examples of "sending."

Near the very beginning of his gospel, John writes that God sent the Baptist into the world for the purpose of bearing witness to the Word or "the light," so that all people might believe through him (1:6-7). God's action in sending the Baptist prefigures his action of sending his own Son into the world (1:9; 3:17; 5:24; etc.). The one act of sending prepares the way for the other, just as, on the human level, the Baptist's witness prepares the way for the coming of Jesus. The relation of John the Baptist to Jesus, conversely, has its source in the nature of God as a God who sends and thereby enters into new relationship with those who are sent as well as with the world into which they are sent. As John the Baptist himself was sent by God, he can testify authentically to Jesus as the Son sent from the Father. In a similar way, because Jesus sends the disciples into the world as the Father has sent him, the disciples become recipients of the action of sending and so can bear authentic witness to Jesus as the Son sent from the Father.

God's own action of sending expresses and deepens his commitment to his world. As Creator of the world, God already stands in a positive relationship to the world and to those who will become believers. As a God who engages in the act of sending, he confirms his relationship with his creation. God is not content simply to observe the world; rather, he assumes an active responsibility for it by sending the Baptist, and then his own Son, into the world. By expressing itself in his acts of sending, God's initial relationship to the world becomes more specific and intentional. All those who are sent -- the Baptist, the Son, and believers -- become beneficiaries of this new relation that God has established with the world. They enter into it and work within it, as the Baptist testifies to Jesus, the Son brings eternal life for all who believe, and believers bear witness to the salvation that their Lord has made available.

John suggests, paradoxically, that the purpose of God's acts of "sending" can be viewed in the broadest possible terms or, at other times, in more limited ways. God sent the Baptist (1:6), who came in order that (*hina*) all people (*pantes*) might believe (1:7). This purpose seems to extend in principle to all the world, so that ultimately all people throughout the world could come to believe in Jesus as a result of the movement initiated by the Baptist. In this vein John describes Jesus as "the true light, which enlightens everyone" (1:9), and as "the Lamb of God who takes away the sin of the world" (1:29). Elsewhere, however, John writes as if the Baptist had a more limited purpose, for he says that the Baptist came baptizing with water in order that Jesus "might be revealed to Israel" (1:31). In this respect Jesus is depicted as fulfilling the specific expectations of the Old Testament and the Jewish faith. Although these two ways of stating the Baptist's purpose do not necessarily conflict with each other, they do seem to represent two different ways of perceiving the scope of his work.

In a similar way, John writes that God sent his Son into the world "in order that (*hina*) the world might be saved through him" (3:17). Here again, God's action seems to have a purpose that extends to the entire world. At the same time, John suggests that in practical terms God's purpose finds expression within a more restricted sphere. In 3:16, which is parallel in structure and meaning to 3:17, John indicates that God "so loved the world" that he gave his Son in order that (*hina*) "everyone who believes in him may not perish but may have eternal life." At this point John speaks of God's purpose in a more limited sense, referring to believers rather than the world *in toto*. Even in 3:16, however, John begins his sentence by speaking of God's love for the world.

The rather puzzling way in which John speaks of God's purpose -- in terms of the world, on the one hand, and in terms of Israel or believers, on the other -- may be a reflection of the empirical fact that many people in the world failed to respond when God sent the Baptist and then his own Son. In this sense John may be formulating his statement of God's purpose with reference to the actual degree of fulfillment that it was receiving, from Jesus' time up to his own. John, it would seem, feels that he must take account of the divided response that the Christian message has received, as some people accept it and others do not.

On a theological level, another explanation is also possible. John may well wish to indicate that God's love for the world always forms the context for his love for believers. God's love for the world establishes the setting in which he loves believers, and his love for the world continues to obtain even when he focuses his love empirically on believers. Conversely, God's actions of "sending," with the purpose of giving salvation and eternal life to all who believe, must always be seen as an aspect of his actions and intentions with reference to the world itself. In this respect John would agree with the comment of J. Edward Dirks, who once remarked that God does not love the world because he loves the church, but he loves the church because he loves the world.[28]

Relation analysis of the concept of "sending" also calls attention to parallels among the relationships that come into being for those who are sent. God sent John the Baptist, for example, and the Baptist gave testimony to Jesus as the light, who ranks ahead of him (1:6-8, 15). Later the Jews sent messengers to the Baptist, and he gave essentially the same testimony to Jesus: "Among you stands one whom you do not know, the one who is coming after me; I am not worthy to untie the thong of his sandal" (1:26-27).

The Baptist persisted in giving this testimony whether or not external conditions were favorable, and he clearly wanted to make it the basis of any relationship that he would have with the Jews who were inquiring about him.

In this respect the Baptist's testimony to the Jews may be seen as a model for the disciples' testimony to the world. As the Baptist made his testimony to Jesus the sole basis for any relationship that he would or would not have with the Jews, so believers must persist in bearing authentic witness to Jesus as the basis for any relationship that they establish with the world. At least in the first instance, they can not relate to the world on any other basis, such as its technology or culture, no matter how worthwhile these may be in themselves. Believers must first relate to the world by bearing witness to Jesus, and only in light of this witness can they develop a broader relationship that may recognize worth in the life of the world, with its own learning, wisdom, and value systems.

As John the Baptist prepared the way for the coming of Jesus, so God's action in sending the Baptist prefigured his sending of his own Son into the world. The preceding analysis has called attention to parallels between these two acts of sending, especially with regard to God's purpose that received expression through these occurrences. God's action in sending his Son, in turn, is correlated with the Son's own action in sending his disciples into the world. The relationship is expressed in the terms "as... so," as in the words of the risen Lord to his followers, "As the Father has sent me, so I send you" (20:21). It is especially helpful at this point to analyze these acts of sending with regard to the results that follow. When the Father sends the Son, for example, what does this mean for the Son himself, for the Son's activities in the world, and for people or believers in the world? How do these results carry over, as it were, to characterize the Son's own action in sending out his disciples, so that the pattern "as... so" is completed?

These questions are important precisely because John says so little about the nature of the mission that the disciples are to undertake in the world. He simply writes that Jesus sends the disciples as the Father has sent him (20:21). The passage corresponds to the "Great Commission" at the close of the Gospel of Matthew, except that Matthew is much more specific: the risen Lord not only sends the disciples to all nations, but instructs them to baptize and to teach, and also assures them of his own continuing presence (Matt. 28:18-20). Throughout his gospel, of course, Matthew has given extensive accounts of Jesus' teaching as examples of the kind of instruction that the disciples can use and transmit in their own work in the world. John, in contrast, says relatively little about the actual work of the disciples or the specific teaching that they are to give. He chooses to focus, rather, on the correlation between the Father's action in sending the Son and the Son's own action in sending the disciples.

In using the terms "as...so" to express this correlation, John seems to reverse a type of argument that Jesus himself had used, according to the synoptic gospels. Jesus sometimes argued from the realm of human experience to the world of divine reality, employing a method of argument that Jewish rabbis called "from light to heavy." In the Sermon on the Mount, for example, Jesus asked, "If you then, who are evil, know how to give good gifts to your children, how much more will your Father in heaven give good things to those who ask him!" (Matt. 7:11; cf. Lk. 11:13). In spite of human imperfection, Jesus was teaching, it is possible to find examples of goodness in human life which do give some idea what God's much greater goodness is like. In this qualified sense it is possible to argue from the human to the divine, looking at the best in human life and then on this basis making inferences about God's own nature. In the thirteenth century Thomas Aquinas continued to employ this "principle of analogy," or *analogia entis*, analogy of being. Thinking about human fathers, for example, helps in understanding the belief that God is Father. The first is an analogy for the second, indicating some similarities which can be carried over from one to the other, even though the correspondence is not exact or complete.

John, in contrast, prefers to think in the other direction, looking first at God's action in sending his Son and then correlating this with the Son's own action in sending believers into the world. In using the terms "as... so," John employs a method of "reverse analogy" that seeks to identify appropriate similarities or correspondences that carry over from the first act of sending to the second. From this perspective John asks what it means to be sent into the world, first for the Son himself and then for the disciples. It becomes especially important to examine John's perspective at this point since otherwise he gives so little information about his understanding of the mission of the disciples to the world.

When John speaks of the Father's sending the Son into the world, it is significant first of all that he thinks of the Father as continuing to be with the Son. "Sending," paradoxically, involves continuing relationship and uninterrupted presence rather than separation. Thus Jesus can declare, "And the one who sent me is with me; he has not left me alone, for I always do what is pleasing to him" (8:29). In the preceding verse Jesus has just alluded to his own death, through the imagery of being "lifted up" as Son of man (8:28). This allusion makes it very likely that he is thinking now of the Father's presence with him throughout his life -- even at the time of his death, when he would be tempted most strongly to feel deserted by God. In a similar vein Jesus refers later to the Father's continuing presence with him even at the "hour" when the disciples will have deserted him (16:32). As the divine Son, Jesus is certain that the Father who sent him always remains with him, providing a sense of presence, reassurance, and support.

Since Jesus sends the disciples as the Father has sent him, it would follow that John thinks of Jesus as continuing to remain with the disciples after he has sent them into the world. "Sending," again, involves the paradox of continuing presence rather than separation. Thus Jesus, looking forward to the post-resurrection period, can reassure his followers of his continuing presence with them as risen Lord: "I will not leave you orphaned; I am coming to you" (14:18). As the presence of the Father with the Son means that the Son does what is pleasing to the Father (8:29), so the presence of Jesus with his followers means that they love him and keep his commandments (14:21, 23). It also means that Jesus loves them, the Father loves them, and Jesus and the Father make their "home" with them (14:21-24). In all these ways, Jesus assures his followers of a profound and sustaining divine presence as he sends them into the world. For both Jesus and the disciples, being sent into the world involves continuing relationship with the one who sends.

If the act of "sending" involves continuing presence, the further question may be raised how God's sending the Son has consequences for the activities that the Son undertakes in the world. When the Father sends the

Son, that is, what results does this action have with regard to the mission of word and deed that the Son himself carries out in the world? The pattern of "as... so," in turn, will suggest that John views this mission as a paradigm for the work of the disciples when they are sent into the world.

In this regard John indicates first that God's action of sending the Son means that the Son speaks the words of the Father: "He whom God has sent speaks the words of God, for he gives the Spirit without measure" (3:34; cf. 5:25; 8:26). The connection between "sending" and "speaking" is enriched at this point by the reference to the Spirit, evidently with the meaning that the Spirit, sent by the Father, continually guides and inspires the activity of the Son in speaking the words of the Father. From a slightly different point of view, John emphasizes that the Son does not attempt to give his own teaching but commits himself to communicating the truth that he has received from the Father: "My teaching is not mine," Jesus asserts, "but his who sent me" (7:16; cf. 12:49; 14:24; 17:8). In this connection John records a very practical test for deciding whether the Son is bringing authentic teaching from the Father: "Anyone who resolves to do the will of God will know whether the teaching is from God or whether I am speaking on my own" (7:17). The intention to act on the basis of truth, John suggests, aids in the perception of truth itself.

The mission of Jesus, as the Son sent by the Father, consists of word and deed. His mission of "word" is to speak the words of God and give God's teaching rather than his own. In a similar way his mission of "deed" is to do the will of God and carry out this will rather than his own. "My food," Jesus explains, "is to do the will of him who sent me and to complete his work" (4:34). Jesus' commitment to doing the will of God is so complete that he can not think in terms of developing a divergent will of his own (5:30; 6:38). In this sense he "can do nothing" on his own (5:30). The "will" of the Father that the Son seeks to carry out is a redemptive will: "This is indeed the will of my Father, that all who see the Son and believe in him may have eternal life; and I will raise them up on the last day" (6:40).

As the Son sent by the Father, Jesus commits himself to a mission of word and deed -- speaking the words of God and doing the will of God. It is intrinsic to this mission, John indicates, that Jesus is seeking the glory of God rather than his own glory. This concern becomes, indeed, a sign of the authenticity of Jesus himself and the work that he undertakes. "Those who speak on their own," Jesus explains, "seek their own glory; but the one who seeks the glory of him who sent him is true, and there is nothing false in him" (7:18). Because the Son seeks only the glory of the Father, the work of the Son in the world is both genuine in itself and genuine as it is perceived by those who believe.

As the Father has sent the Son, so the Son sends the disciples into the world (17:18; 20:21). John is thinking in terms of reverse analogy, according to the pattern of "as... so" (kathōs...kai), in the belief that salient characteristics of the first act of sending will also apply to the second. According to this way of thinking, the disciples would also receive a mission of word and deed that is modeled after Jesus' own mission. As the Father sent the Son to speak the words of God and give God's teaching rather than his own, so it would follow that the Son sends believers into the world to communicate the Son's words and transmit his teaching rather than their own. As the Father sent the Son to do the will of God and carry out this will rather than his own, so it would follow that the Son sends the disciples into the world to do his will and carry out this will rather than their own. Finally, as Jesus sought the glory of the Father who sent him, so the disciples would seek the glory of the one who sent them, rather than their own glory. These characteristics of the work of the disciples in the world would all be valid according to the "as... so" pattern of reasoning that John follows.

There is no reason to question that John does indeed think of the mission of the disciples in these terms. The very fact that he calls attention to the "as... so" type of analogy (17:18; 20:21) suggests that he regards Jesus' own mission as the model for a comparable mission on the part of believers. It should be noted, however, that John establishes a connection between the idea of "sending" and a description of "mission" only when he is exploring the significance of the Father's action in sending the Son. He does not make this connection, or give a description of mission, when he is speaking of the Son's own action of sending believers into the world. Perhaps John assumes at this point that his readers will complete the comparison for themselves: they will be able to think in terms of reverse analogy and perceive the similarity between the work of the Son and the work of the disciples in the world.

John does, in fact, give some description of the life that the disciples will lead after Jesus has returned to the Father, although he does not link this description with the concept of "sending." The disciples, for instance, are to love one another (13:34; 15:12, 17). They will bear much "fruit" (15:5-8) and will do the works that Jesus does and even greater works than these (14:12). They will keep Jesus' commandments (14:15, 21, 23). They will have spiritual union with Jesus (14:20, 23; 15:4-8), and they will abide in Jesus' love (15:9-10) and in the Father's love (17:26). They will be "friends" of Jesus (15:13-15), experiencing peace (14:27; 16:33) and joy (15:11; 16:20-24; 17:13). The disciples will receive continuing instruction from the Holy Spirit (14:26; 16:13), and they will receive from the Father whatever they ask in Jesus' name (15:16; 16:23). The disciples, finally, are to testify on behalf of Jesus (15:27) and bring others to faith in him (17:20).

This description of the life of the early Christian community, as important as it is, focuses almost entirely on the internal life of the community itself. It includes very little concerning the content or structure of the mission of the disciples to the world around them. For this reason it is especially important to supplement John's description with the principle, based on the "as... so" pattern of reasoning, that the disciples, like Jesus himself, are sent into the world with a mission of word and deed, witness and work. Only with this mission in mind could John have recorded Jesus' words, "As the Father has sent me, so I send you" (20:21). In this regard the methodology of relation analysis helps to identify the importance that John attaches to the theme of mission, even though he touches on this theme only briefly in his description of the early Christian community.

The method of relation analysis can examine God's action of sending the Son into the world with regard to the results of this action as they pertain to the Son himself, the mission that he undertakes, the disciples who receive a mission of their own, or the people in the world generally. The investigation so far has focused on the results of God's action as they affect the Son, his mission, and the disciples. It is appropriate now to ask how God's action of sending the Son affected the people in the world, and how this particular result may be correlated with the work of the disciples in the world. These questions are important because John actually says very little about the content of the message that the disciples are to bring or the new possibilities of faith that their message will bring to the world.

When the Father sent the Son into the world, John suggests that the major consequence for the people in the world was the opportunity to receive eternal life. According to one of the central passages in the gospel, people can receive this gift through hearing the word of the Son and believing the Father who sent him: "Very truly, I tell you," Jesus explains, "anyone who hears my word and believes him who sent me has eternal life, and does not come under judgment, but has passed from death to life" (5:24). In a number of other passages also, John establishes this connection between the Father's action of sending and the gift of salvation or eternal life (3:17; 6:39-40, 57; 17:3). Although God's intention to give this gift goes back at least to the creation of the world (1:4), it was his action of sending the Son that made the reception of the gift a concrete possibility for people in the world.

In other ways also John makes a connection between God's action of sending his Son and the consequences of this action for people in the world. If people would believe the Son, for example, they would have a greater knowledge of the Father who sent him (5:37-38; cf. 7:28-29). When people do believe in the Son, they are believing in the Father who sent him (12:44). Similarly, when they see the Son, they see the Father who sent him (12:45). In these ways the Father's action of sending the Son makes it possible for the Son to make known the Father (cf. 1:18).

In making this connection between the events of "sending" and "knowing," John clearly wishes to define the conditions under which the first occurrence leads to the second. If people are to receive knowledge of the Father, it is necessary first that they believe in the Son who is sent from the Father. They must be able to "see" the Son with the eyes of faith if they are to "see" the Father. Without this response of faith, the revelation of the Father in the Son remains hidden. Secondly, when people do respond by believing in the Son, they receive a mediate rather than a direct knowledge of the Father. They do not pass from one stage to another -- from "seeing" the Son to "seeing" the Father -- but they always see the Father through seeing the Son, and they always know the Father as he is made known in the Son. This knowledge of the Father, John seems to suggest, is no less real or life-giving because it is mediated through the Son. It is sufficient in itself for those who believe, and it continues to characterize the connection between the concepts of "sending" and "knowing."

At this point the method of relation analysis, following John's pattern of "as... so," suggests that the consequences of the one act of sending also apply to the other. As the Father's action of sending the Son had certain consequences for people in the world, so the Son's action of sending disciples is to have similar consequences for those in the world. The Father's action of sending results in the message that those who believe in the Father and the Son may receive the gift of eternal life and may know the Father through the Son. In a very similar way the Son's own action of sending out disciples means that the disciples are to bring the same message to the world. They too are to proclaim that those who respond in faith may receive the gift of eternal life and may come to know the Father in the Son. As the Father sent the Son to bring this life-giving and revelatory message to the world, so the Son sends the disciples to continue to communicate the same message.

John's perspective of reverse analogy applies to the activities that believers undertake in the world as well as to the conceptual message that they bring. As the Father sent the Son for a ministry of word and deed, so the Son sends the disciples for a comparable mission of word and deed in the world. The works that the Son accomplishes testify that the Father sent him (5:36; cf. 11:42). These works result from the Father's action of sending. At the same time, they serve to confirm it because they always remain true to the Father's own purpose of expressing his redemptive love through the ministry of his Son in the world.

When Jesus reminds believers that they will do the works that he does (14:12), it is important to recognize that these works stand in a relation of "as... so" to Jesus' own works. Whatever specific activities of mission or service believers may undertake, their works result from the fact that Jesus has sent them into the world. Their works, furthermore, are authentic to the extent that they give expression to Jesus' own gracious and redemptive purposes for the world. As the Son carried out a ministry that brought honor to the Father (8:49), so believers are commissioned to undertake a ministry of word and deed that will remain true to the will of the one who sent them (cf. 12:26).

To alert the reader to significant features of the narrative world that he is presenting, John focuses at this point on relationships, omission, and paradox. In depicting relationships, he calls attention especially to correlations, expressed by the "as... so" pattern of thought. These stimulate the reader to think in terms of the principle of reverse analogy, so that the reader can perceive more clearly the correspondences between the Father's sending the Son, and the Son's sending the disciples. When John refers to Jesus' action of sending the disciples into the world, he noticeably omits to describe their mission of word and deed, witness and service. He wants the reader again to think in terms of reverse analogy, recognizing that the ministry of the Son serves at this point as a paradigm for the ministry that the disciples receive. When John develops the theme of "sending," he presents the paradox that the one who sends maintains a continual presence with the one who is sent. Just as the Father sends the Son but remains with the Son, so the Son sends believers into the world but always sustains them by his continual presence as the risen Lord. By focusing in this way on relationships, omission, and paradox, John invites the reader to reflect on the meaning of the text as part of the total process of actualizing or completing the text.

CHAPTER V

Author and Readers: The Communication of Faith

A. Loci of Revelation

In the biblical tradition generally the term "revelation" means that God discloses something about himself or the world that people would not be able to know merely by using their own processes of reasoning or their faculties of spiritual perception. God may reveal some aspect of himself, such as his presence, his love, or his will. In this case God becomes both the subject and the object of revelation. Or God may disclose religious truths or ethical teachings, making them known and at the same time giving them the authority of divine revelation. In this instance God remains the subject of divine revelation, but the object is stated in conceptual form.

Whether God reveals himself or some conceptual principle, the idea of revelation signifies that God makes something known which the human mind or heart could not perceive by itself. Even if people can learn something about God by reflecting, for example, on the natural world, the idea of revelation means that they can do so only because God has first revealed something of himself in the world. Thus the writer of Psalm 19, for instance, does not use the natural world as the basis for a philosophical proof of the existence of God, but does affirm that creation testifies to God's glory (Ps. 19:1-4).

In contrast to Paul (Rom. 1:19-20; 3:14-16) and Luke (Acts 17:24-29), who evidently believed in the possibility of receiving some limited knowledge of God from reflection on the created world, John shows very little interest in this kind of "general revelation." He prefers to begin with the assumption that "no one has ever seen God," and then he emphasizes that the only Son, the incarnate Word, "has made him known" (1:18). Even when he thinks in broad terms about humanity in general, John focuses on the Word, who was "the true light, which enlightens everyone..." (1:9). In contrast to any theory of general revelation through the order of creation or the structures of human experience, John prefers to emphasize the unique role of the Son, the incarnate Word, in revealing God.

This emphasis on the Word signifies that John is thinking specifically in terms of revelation within history. The Word becomes incarnate in Jesus Christ and lives a human life (1:14), offering "grace and truth" to people (1:17). For John, the concept of revelation refers, at least in the first instance, to the incarnation, ministry, death, resurrection, and ascension of Jesus as the Word of God. These occurrences all together constitute the primary revelatory event in history. Any other way of thinking of revelation, John implies, must be secondary to this perception of the revelatory function of the Word. The significance of any other form of revelation, further, must always be measured in relation to the Word itself.

If the term "revelation," for John, refers primarily to Jesus himself as the Word of God, it is also possible to ask whether it can have secondary or derivative meanings. The term could apply, for example, to the deeds and teachings of Jesus during his earthly ministry, since these help people learn about God and his will for human life. With regard to the role of John himself, the idea of revelation could include John's understanding of Jesus and his ministry, on the assumption that God was actively involved at this point in helping John perceive the significance of Jesus as the incarnate Word.

Since John recorded his insights in written form, the concept of revelation could also apply to the Gospel of John as a written text. With regard to those who read the gospel, revelation could have reference to the process of reading, in the sense that God may guide the readers in understanding the meaning of the text. As a final stage, the term "revelation" may be applicable if God helps readers in the process of constructive reading, entering into engagement with the text and fulfilling or actualizing its meaning.

In theory, at least, it is possible to identify these six ways of thinking about revelation. The first way, for John, is always primary, because of his emphasis on the role of the Word in making God known. The following five are derivative, each one dependent, not only on the first, but on all those that precede. On the assumption that God may be actively involved at any stage, the idea of revelation could refer to all these points or *loci*:

1. Jesus himself, as the Word of God

2. Jesus' deeds and teachings during his earthly ministry, in his role as incarnate Word (1)

3. John's own understanding of the meaning of Jesus and his ministry (1, 2)

4. The Gospel of John as a written text, expressing John's understanding of Jesus (3)

5. The readers' perception of the meaning of the Gospel of John as a written text (4)

6. The readers' engagement with the text, fulfilling or actualizing its meaning (5).

The concept of revelation seems simple at first, when John writes that no one has ever seen God but the only Son has made him known (1:18). The idea becomes more complex, however, when the possibility is raised that God may actively involve himself in subsequent stages of the process by which John writes his gospel and then other people read it. This understanding of revelation means, for example, that author, text, and reader all have a role to play in the total process by which God makes himself known to people. Although the concept of revelation focuses on the Word of God, the whole process of communicating revelation also becomes important.

John's emphasis on the Word of God also provides perspective for assessing the idea of "continuing revelation," which implies that distinctly new revelation or new truth is disclosed at some later point. To say that God may be involved in the process by which revelation is communicated from author to reader is not necessarily to endorse the concept of continuing revelation. John's focus on the Word of God as the primary datum of revelation suggests that God's subsequent involvement in the process of transmitting this revelation would lead to a clearer understanding of revelation through the Word rather than to new revelation *per se*.

With regard to the present study, it is important note that the role of revelation, in theological terms, is parallel to the role of meaning, in literary terms. Just as the question may be raised at what point revelation occurs in the process of writing and reading a gospel, so the similar question may be raised at what point meaning arises in the process of composing and reading a literary work. Just as the idea of revelation may be applicable to several stages in the process of writing and reading a gospel, so the idea of meaning may refer to several stages in the production and interpretation of a literary work. Just as one form of revelation may be primary, so that other types of revelation must be assessed by their relation to it, so meaning may arise in a primary way at some particular point in the process of writing and reading a literary work, with the result that other forms of meaning must be measured by their congruence with this primary meaning. Since the Gospel of John is both a gospel and a literary work, it will be important to correlate these concepts of "revelation" and "meaning."

B. Author, Text, and Reader

Interpreters of Scripture and readers of literary works have often assumed that an author had specific ideas in mind and then wrote a text in order to communicate these ideas to readers. The emphasis in this view falls on the concepts or intentions that the author originally had in mind. These constitute the revelation or meaning that the author wished to transmit. The author had an active role in this process, formulating ideas and then stating them in written form. The text becomes a medium for communicating the author's intention. As a bridge between author and readers, it is relatively unimportant in itself. Although readers may be actively engaged in reading the text carefully, they are really passive in the sense that their purpose is to receive the meaning that the author wished to communicate through the text.

Whether they are specifically trained in the interpretation of Scripture or the study of literature, many readers today probably share this viewpoint. They regard it as logical that the author's intention should be of primary importance -- i.e., an author writes to communicate ideas, and readers then read to understand these ideas. In biblical study this approach recalls the early school of Antioch, with its concern for the literal sense of a text, in contrast to the method of allegorical interpretation more popular at Alexandria, which gave more scope to the constructive interpretation of the reader. This approach is reminiscent too of the viewpoint of Thomas Aquinas in the thirteenth century, who rejected the predominant methodology of allegorical interpretation in favor of an emphasis on the literal meaning of Scripture.

This author-centered approach also reflects the influence of the Renaissance scholars who sought to use their knowledge of ancient languages, textual criticism, and historical background to identify the meaning that an author wished to communicate in a text. It is compatible also with the Reformation insistence that the ideas and faith expressed in the Bible should be normative for the life of the church. The word "exegesis" -- literally, "leading out" -- epitomizes this view that the first task of biblical study is always to discover the meaning that the writer originally wished to convey to the readers.

Recent trends in literary criticism and biblical study (e.g., the New Criticism, reader-response theory, structuralism, deconstruction) have moved critical attention away from the role of the author. In one way or another, these schools regard it as unnecessary or even impossible to identify the intention of the individual author as part of the process of interpreting the meaning of a text. Yet it may also be relevant at this point to recall "what C.S. Lewis called the chronological fallacy -- the belief that because something is not currently fashionable, it cannot be true."[29] Somehow the reader still approaches the text with the assumption that the author had something to communicate. From a theological standpoint, as it was noted above, one meaning of "revelation" is that God may guide the biblical writer in the whole process of understanding the subject matter and communicating it to the reader. From this theological perspective, therefore, it can still be meaningful to seek to recover the original meaning that an author wished to convey.

As Edgar Krentz has written in his survey of the historical-critical method, "The historian uses all the linguistic tools available to determine the meaning the text had for its first hearers at the time of original composition (intended sense)."[30] Krentz remains convinced that the historical-critical method will continue to be basic in biblical interpretation-i.e., interpreters will continue to ask what meaning the author originally intended to convey to the first readers. It is interesting to note, at the same time, that Krentz also speaks of the need for this method to be supplemented by others, such as "literary history," which "concentrates on the actual work of literature as an entity in itself."[31]

In literary theory the "New Criticism" represents exactly this emphasis on the work of literature as an organic unity in itself. Developed by literary critics in England and America in the 1940's, this method assumes that the literary text should be interpreted as an entity in itself, with special attention to "objective" aspects such as structure, figures of speech, and the organic connection between form and content. The New Criticism gives its attention to the work of literature itself, rather than seeking to discover the intentions of the author or the setting in which the text was produced (e.g., biographical, historical, sociological, philosophical). In a similar way it seeks to avoid the "affective fallacy" of taking into account the subject perceptions of the reader. Terence J. Keegan has suggested that this concern for objectivity in the New Criticism reflects the influence of scientific positivism, with its assumption that the results of an experiment can be measured with objective certitude.[32]

As a methodology, the New Criticism shows similarities to several types of biblical study. It has some parallel, for instance, to form criticism, which is also concerned with the structure of a text and the close relation between form and content. It shows some similarity as well to canonical criticism, which, in one of its forms, analyzes the meaning of a biblical document as it was "stabilized" at the critical point of becoming canonical. Both form criticism and canonical criticism, however, have some diachronic interest in the pre-history of the written text, and both are especially interested in the function of the text (or the materials that make up the text) within the life of the faith community. In these respects the New Criticism, with its focus on objective interpretation of the text in itself, shows no parallels to form or canonical criticism.

Recently Stephen D. Moore has argued that the difference between composition criticism (with its concern for a separable theological content) and narrative criticism (in which meaning is inseparable from form) must be understood in relation to the tenets of the New Criticism.[33] This perception illustrates another way in which the influence of the New Criticism may be felt in biblical studies. In a similar vein, Robert Kysar speaks of the "poetic power" of "true metaphors" to create a new experience or reality that would be impossible without them. These true or poetic metaphors (i.e., diaphors) may be distinguished from ordinary metaphors (i.e., epiphors) that serve simply as vehicles for truth and have, presumably, a separable theological content.[34] With respect to the Gospel of John, Kysar writes, "Indeed, the entire Gospel of John might be considered an extended metaphor in which the author is trying less to communicate some universal truths through individual narratives and speeches than create a reader experience of a world at the center of which stands the Christ figure."[35]

These observations concerning narrative criticism and "true metaphors" or "diaphors" are parallel to the New Critical principle of an organic connection between the form and the content of a literary work. In this respect they illustrate once again the continuing influence of the New Criticism in interpretive methodologies. In a more general sense, the influence of the New Criticism helps biblical interpreters appreciate the intrinsic importance of the text as a literary work and recognize the need for careful attention to features such as structure and figures of speech.

As the New Criticism moved critical interest from the author to the literary work itself, so reader-response criticism has shifted attention from the text as a self-contained entity to the reader who brings the literary work to completion through the act of reading. The New Criticism assumed that readers of a literary work, through careful and objective analysis, would all arrive at substantially the same understanding of its meaning. In this way the

New Criticism minimized or ignored the individual reactions and interpretations of readers. Developed in the 1960's as a literary theory and applied in the 1970's to biblical interpretation, the methodology of reader-response criticism has sought to call attention to the critical importance of the act of reading in the process by which meaning is produced.

Two illustrations in recent publications call attention to some important aspects of reader-response criticism. In his book on biblical hermeneutics, Terence J. Keegan suggests that a message can be communicated only if it is received. When a tree falls down in the forest, it does not, strictly speaking, make a "sound." It produces wave patterns of condensed and rarefied air, but these patterns themselves are not sound. They produce the sensation of sound only when they can enter a human ear. If a falling tree is to produce a sound, a listener must be present. In a similar way, Keegan suggests, the Bible has a message to communicate, but it can communicate this message only when the message is received. A reader must be present to receive the message and make meaning out of the biblical text.[36]

The second illustration is perhaps more complex. A cartoon on the cover of *Reader-Response Criticism: From Formalism to Post-Structuralism*, edited by Jane P. Tompkins, depicts three people standing, evidently in a subway car, and holding on to straps extending from the roof of the car. The woman in the middle is reading a book. The two men on either side are looking over her shoulder and reading the book too. One of the men is weeping, with large tears falling down to the floor. The other one is amused, with his mouth wide open in hearty laughter. The cartoon shows two readers, reading the same text but showing very different reactions.

This illustration calls attention to three aspects of reader-response criticism. It suggests, first, that a text is actualized or brought to completion only through the act of reading. Before it is read, the text is a "virtual entity," a potentiality, but it must be read to be actualized. The two men in the cartoon are actively involved in reading the text and bringing it to actuality as a literary work.

The cartoon points out, secondly, that readers may react in different ways to the same text. In this case one reader finds it distressing and the other sees it as highly amusing. Because the readers themselves contribute to the meaning of the text, they may bring it to completion in different ways.

As a result of this variation in response, the cartoon calls attention, thirdly, to the question of hermeneutical control that must be raised in connection with the method of reader-response criticism. The two men give different responses. Is one response as "correct" or "valid" as the other? Would any other response be as "right" as these two? Could a response be "wrong"? Are readers free to find any meaning they wish in the text? If reader-response criticism is not interested -- or not primarily interested -- in discerning the intention of the author or analyzing the text as a literary work, then it must address the question of identifying principles of interpretation governing the meanings that readers find or produce in the act of reading.

Reader-response critics are indeed aware of this issue, even if they have different ways of understanding the activity of the reader and different views of the extent to which readers are subject to interpretive norms. Peter J. Rabinowitz has suggested that most reader-response critics "would probably agree that on some level readers 'construe' or 'construct' meaning."[37] To "construe" meaning is to "decode" or "realize" a text by responding to cues within the text itself. Thus Wolfgang Iser, for example, speaks of "gaps" in the text that must be filled in by the reader. These serve, in fact, to direct the reader to respond in certain ways. In this respect it is significant that the text continues to exert an influence, even in reader-response criticism.[38]

To "construct" the meaning of a text, in contrast, means that the reader plays a more active role, developing an interpretation in terms of his or her own individuality that may differ substantially from the interpretations offered by other readers. Rabinowitz refers to David Bleich as an example of a critic who stresses this subjective nature of the reading process.[39] In between these extremes of "construing" or "constructing" meaning, Rabinowitz also mentions critics, such as Jonathan Culler and Stanley Fish, who stress that interpretation of a text takes place within the context of community norms -- socially determined conventions and strategies of reading.[40]

With reference specifically to biblical study, Terence J. Keegan reflects an awareness of these same issues and problems. He takes the position that the creative activity of the reader actualizes a text and give it its full meaning.[41] Yet he also sees the individual reader as a self living in a social context and constrained by a particular value system. The reader is not free to assign any meaning at all to a given text, because he or she can not function as a completely autonomous individual apart from involvement in some value system.[42]

Keegan stresses that the implied reader of a biblical text must be a member of the faith community, the church, because the text conveys a specific ideology and presupposes a reader who can affirm this ideology. In a similar way the real reader who enters into engagement with the text can assume the role of the implied reader only as a member of the same faith community. Using the Gospel of Matthew as an example, Keegan writes, "Apart from being a member of the Christian community, one cannot accept the role required of the implied reader of the text, i.e., one simply cannot read the Gospel of Matthew. One can analyze it as a scientist, but one cannot read it and receive from it its intended effect."[43] In this way, Keegan believes, the method of reader-response criticism helps restore the Bible to the church, and the church in turn provides a context that guards against extremes of subjective interpretation.[44]

C. Relation Analysis and Reader Response

The first part of this chapter (Section A) described different ways in which the concept of "revelation" can be understood, beginning with Jesus himself as the incarnate Word, and extending through Jesus' earthly ministry, John's understanding of Jesus, the Gospel of John as a written text, the reader's understanding of the meaning of the text, and the reader's actualization of the text through the act of reading. "Revelation" may occur at any of these points if God is active at any of them, disclosing divine truth and enriching the understanding of human beings at critical points in the whole process of writing and reading a text. Since John regards the Word of God as the primary datum of revelation, his understanding of Jesus as the incarnate Word must provide the criterion by which the other *loci* of revelation can be assessed and measured.

The second part of this chapter (Section B) discussed ways in which "meaning" may be understood in literary theory. The history of interpretation suggested that "meaning" may be equivalent to the author's intention, or it may inhere in the text itself, or it may be actualized in the process of reading, as readers "construe" or "construct" meaning. Meaning is parallel to revelation in the sense that both may refer to different stages in the process leading from author to reader. With regard to the final stage of this process -- the stage that analyzes the role of the reader -- meaning and revelation are also parallel in the sense that the question must be raised whether any interpretive norms provide external constraints on the subjective responses of the reader.

In light of these analyses of "revelation" and "meaning," this section of the chapter will ask how John, as an author, communicates with his readers. More precisely, it will ask how John, as the real author, assumes the role of implied author in order to communicate his faith to implied readers, in the hope that his real readers will assume the role of the implied readers and in this way affirm the reality of the narrative world that he is presenting. Historical-critical scholars may not know who "John" was, as the real author or school of writers and editors who actually produced the gospel. Literary critics can think of John as the implied author who placed in the text the particular set of values and beliefs that come to expression in the text. To the extent that implied readers stand within the text, they share the values and beliefs of the text and fill in its gaps to complete its narrative world. Implied readers also point beyond the text to the real readers, who are challenged to grow in faith and self-understanding by accepting the ideology and narrative world of the implied readers.

As the implied author, John communicates a network of relationships to his implied readers. These relationships involve the Father, the Son, and the Spirit; God and believers; believers and believers; and believers and the world. In their totality, these relationships constitute the narrative world that John wishes to present to his readers. It would be an example of the "referential fallacy" to assume that these relationships actually existed, as

John presents them, in Jesus' time, John's time, or the reader's own day. John is not trying to make this claim, although, from a theological perspective, he would want to affirm the intrinsic reality of relationships among the persons of the Godhead, and he would also want to affirm that God, as a loving God, always stands ready to initiate and sustain relationships with people. John's main concern in his gospel is to delineate these relationships for their own sake, as the narrative world which his implied readers affirm and his real readers have the opportunity to affirm.

By presenting these relationships to his implied readers, John is also inviting the actual readers to share the faith that the relationships presuppose and enter into the world that they define. This "world" is a world of spiritual reality, in which Christian believers find the meaning of their lives through the relationships that they are privileged to have with God, one another, and human society. This spiritual world of relationships is more "real" than the material, empirical world *per se*, but it always positions itself in, and maintains contact with, the empirical world. The very fact that John presents an account of Jesus' earthly ministry reflects his conviction that this world of relationships always finds its setting in the empirical world of everyday life.[45]

By inviting the actual readers to share the faith that the implied readers accept within the text, John seeks to establish contact with the actual readers. He assumes the role of witness, testifying to the reality of the world of relationships depicted in the text, just as, within the text, the Baptist bears witness to Jesus. Thus John, the implied author, establishes a relationship with his readers that is modeled on the relationship of John the Baptist to Jesus.

John expresses his intention as an author when he depicts relationships to the implied readers, invites the actual readers to enter into the world that these relationships define, and assumes in this way the role of bearing witness. Although advocates of the New Criticism would want to avoid the "intentional fallacy" of giving consideration to the intentions of an author, it would not seem necessary to deny that John, as the implied author of the gospel, could have convictions and purposes of his own. From a literary point of view, these convictions and purposes could affect the meaning of the text, even when interpreters seek to regard the text as an entity in itself. In theological terms, the intention of the author could be an aspect of divine revelation, if it can be assumed that God was aiding John in the whole process of reflecting on the meaning of Jesus' ministry and then constructing the network of relationships that he depicts in his narrative world.

At the same time that John expresses his intention as an author, he also points beyond it by focusing the readers' attention on the relationships that he delineates in his gospel. He wants his readers to be concerned, not simply with his own intention, but with the world of relationships that he has so carefully placed before them. In this way John allows his intention as an author to point beyond itself, or transcend itself, because of the intrinsic importance of his narrative world of relationships.

By emphasizing relationships in this way, John also draws the readers' attention away from the written text to the narrative world that it depicts. In one sense it is true that the text, as an organic entity, can stand by itself, so that it becomes a source of meaning or a vehicle of divine revelation. John wishes, however, to focus attention on the narrative world of relationships within the text, rather than the structure or literary features of the text itself. John's concern for the reality of relationships means that the text transcends itself, just as his own intention as an author transcends itself.

From this perspective it is also possible to assess the significance of reader-response criticism in interpreting the Gospel of John. Reader-response criticism complements relation analysis by emphasizing, in turn, the narrative world that the author has constructed, the implied reader who affirms the reality of this narrative world, and the real reader who is invited to actualize the text by accepting the convictions of the implied reader. The reader actualizes the text of the Gospel of John by appropriating and entering the narrative world of relationships that the methodology of relation analysis has identified.

At the same time, John's concern for the reality of relationships means ultimately that he wishes to stress the critical significance of these relationships themselves rather than any aspect of the writing-reading process. His emphasis on the narrative world of relationships establishes hermeneutical control over all aspects of interpretation, so that the reader, for example, "construes" meaning in the direction of this world rather than in any other direction. Just as John's own intention points beyond itself, and then the written text of the gospel points beyond itself, so John invites the reader ultimately to transcend the act of reading by appropriating the reality of the relationships which the act of reading has made it possible to perceive.

Relation analysis overlaps with reader-response criticism at the point of the narrative world that relation analysis delineates and reader-response criticism invites the reader to affirm. At this point the reader is not a completely autonomous self, free to respond in any way at all to the text. The implied reader responds in the direction of the world of relationships that the text presents, and the actual reader then actualizes the text by responding in the same direction. The Gospel of John places these constraints on the reader's response because John consistently thinks in terms of revelation in history: the Word of God becomes incarnate and makes God known in human history, making possible the network of relationships that the reader may share. If revelation in history places an external constraint on reader response, this constraint in turn becomes a positive benefit by offering the reader the opportunity to affirm a specific set of relationships involving God, believers, and the world.

D. Continuing Concerns

This study of the Gospel of John has argued that relation analysis and reader-response criticism complement one another, in the sense that relation analysis delineates a narrative world of relationships which reader-response criticism then invites the reader to affirm. In this respect the one methodology leads into the other. A number of questions or concerns may be raised, however, about the roles of these methodologies, together and individually. These questions may have some value in the continuing task of biblical study, even if they can not be answered in any definitive way at this point.

A first question concerns the relation of these two methodologies to historical-critical methods of study. In theory, at least, relation analysis and reader-response criticism are synchronic methodologies. They deal with the text as it is, without asking about the historicity of the situations that the text presents or the stages through which the materials passed before reaching their final form. Like other synchronic methodologies, they look at the text as a finished product rather than as a historical source or the result of a developmental process.

In general, these two methods seem to function reasonably well on the plane of synchronic analysis. Occasionally, however, they seem unable to avoid a diachronic interest. Relation analysis, for example, can describe the relationship that John presents between Jesus and Peter. It can identify the aspects that John wishes to emphasize, and it can suggest why John considered these aspects important as part of the entire narrative world that he was constructing. The question may be raised how John's presentation of this relationship differed from the accounts in the synoptic gospels. More importantly, the question may be raised to what extent John's account reflects the relationship that actually existed between Jesus and Peter. These are questions of a comparative and diachronic nature. Perhaps they are inappropriate to synchronic analysis itself. But then a broader theological question arises: if relation analysis has no interest in historical actuality, what happens to revelation in history? The very fact that John thinks so consistently in terms of revelation in history makes it important to raise this question.

The same kind of question arises with regard to reader-response criticism. In itself, this method is concerned only with the narrative world of a text. As a synchronic approach, it has no interest in the historical actuality that the narrative world may reflect. The reader is invited to respond, for example, to the figure of Jesus as part of the narrative world, without regard to the historicity of this figure. But the question may be raised, what happens then to revelation in history if the narrative world of a text has no intrinsic relation to historical actuality.

These concerns about relation analysis and reader-response criticism would probably apply also to any other synchronic methodologies, at least when these methodologies are applied to texts, such as the Bible, which reflect the perspective of revelation in history. Perhaps the basic issue at this point is the question whether a purely synchronic methodology is possible in relation to the principle of historical revelation.

The recent study by Mark W.G. Stibbe -- *John as Storyteller: Narrative Criticism and the Fourth Gospel* -- deserves special attention in this regard. Stibbe believes that narrative criticism has a "synchronic orientation" and also a "diachronic orientation." In the former sense it focuses on "narrative Christology" and "narrative genre." In the latter sense it deals with "community narrative" and "narrative history."[46] Stibbe considers it very important to investigate these diachronic aspects of narrative criticism. Thus he suggests, for example, that "John does refer to facts about Jesus, and... these facts were originally part of a life-history with its own, internal narrativity."[47]

A second set of questions concerns the issue of subjectivity or individualism that is implicit in some forms of reader-response theory. The "reader," for example, may be thought of as an individual person who reads a New Testament text, acquires faith in Christ, and becomes a disciple. Johannes Beutler, in his article in the *Semeia* volume on the Fourth Gospel, has suggested that the Fourth Gospel also emphasizes the importance of topics such as ecclesiology, Christology, and the activity of God in expressing his love for the world.[48]

It is remarkable how similar these concerns are to the questions that were raised some time ago about Rudolf Bultmann's existentialist understanding of the gospel. Did Bultmann put too much emphasis, for example, on the concrete circumstances and experience of the individual believer? Did he see the believer as a member of the community of faith? Did he think of Jesus as bringing an atonement that involved more than a transformation in the self-understanding of the individual believer? Did he think of God as acting in history, moving from a past to a future that were more comprehensive than the past and the future of the believer? The same issues that Beutler calls attention to in his critique of reader-response theory -- ecclesiology, Christology, and the activity of God in history -- are also issues that arise in regard to Bultmann's existentialism.

A final area of interest concerns the application of relation analysis to other writings in the Bible. This methodology arises naturally in the study of the Fourth Gospel, since John himself presents such a rich variety of relationships as structural elements in his narrative. From the very beginning of his gospel, in which he writes that the Word was "with" God, John indicates that he will be thinking in terms of the critical importance of relationships. The question may be raised at this point whether relation analysis would be helpful in the study of other biblical writings, even though their authors may not delineate relationships so clearly.

Would it be possible -- as a concrete example -- to look at the Old Testament book of Amos from the standpoint of relation analysis? The writer certainly does not call attention to relationships or give them extensive development in the way that John does. Yet the reader can identify a number of relationships within the text. These include, for example, the relation between God and Amos, between God and Israel (the covenant people), between God and the two divided kingdoms, between God and various groups within Israel (the rich, the poor, the powerful, the oppressed, etc.), between God and the nations of the world, between Israel and the nations, between Amos and his opponents (such as Amaziah), between Amos and his audience, between Amos and his followers. In each case the interpreter would want to analyze the relationship as it is presented in the text and then ask whether some relationships can be correlated with others. In the case of the last two relationships mentioned above, the interpreter would notice that the text is silent. The text, that is, does not indicate whether Amos met with a favorable response from his audience or attracted a group of followers. The reader, therefore, must seek to explain these silences or gaps in the text.

As this example illustrates, the method of relation analysis will function in somewhat different ways with regard to different writings. Although it is a methodology for approaching the text, it must also have some flexibility in adapting to the structure of a particular text. Its general purpose, in the case of Amos or other biblical writings, is to help the interpreter acquire a clearer understanding of the message of Scripture.

NOTES

Full bibliographical data for each reference are given the first time it is cited in the notes.

[1]R. Alan Culpepper, *Anatomy of the Fourth Gospel: A Study in Literary Design* (Philadelphia: Fortress Press, 1983); Edgar V. McKnight, *Post-Modern Use of the Bible: The Emergence of Reader-Oriented Criticism* (Nashville: Abingdon Press, 1988); Stephen D. Moore, *Literary Criticism and the Gospels: The Theoretical Challenge* (New Haven and London: Yale University Press, 1989); Jeffrey Lloyd Staley, *The Print's First Kiss: A Rhetorical Investigation of the Implied Reader in the Fourth Gospel* (Atlanta, Georgia: Scholars Press, 1988).

[2]Reader-response theory also includes the "narrator" (the "voice" that tells the story) and the "narratee" (the one to whom the narrator tells the story). In a given literary work the narrator and the narratee may, or may not, be clearly distinguished from the implied author and the implied reader, respectively. Culpepper prefers to use the terms narrator and narratee, but he also states that in John these terms can scarcely be distinguished from implied author and implied reader. Cf. *Anatomy of the Fourth Gospel*, pp. 7-8, 16, 43, 206, 232. Staley defines the implied reader as the one who has knowledge of the story only as it is narrated, while the narratee has some knowledge of the story even before it is told. Cf. *The Print's First Kiss*, pp. 44-45. He also states, however, that implied reader and narratee share much of "the same narrative territory" in the Fourth Gospel (*ibid.*, p. 47).

[3]For a discussion of strategies or techniques that the reader may utilize in "actualizing" biblical texts cf. also McKnight, *Post-Modern Use of the Bible*, Chapter 5.

[4]Wolfgang Iser, *The Implied Reader: Patterns of Communication in Prose Fiction from Bunyan to Beckett* (Baltimore and London: The Johns Hopkins University Press, 1974) p. 280.

[5]Culpepper, *Anatomy of the Fourth Gospel*, p. 97. On the importance of responses to Jesus, cf. also pp. 148, 233.

[6]Wolfgang Iser, *The Act of Reading: A Theory of Aesthetic Response* (Baltimore and London: The Johns Hopkins University Press, 1978) p. 19.

[7]One is reminded of the problem whether "equality with God" in Philip. 2:6 should be understood as a status already achieved (*res rapta*) or a status still to be acquired (*res rapienda*). John clearly thinks of Jesus' sonship to God as an existing reality, but then he wishes to emphasize that Jesus' role as Son expresses itself in his redemptive work on behalf of people.

[8]Moody Smith, *Johannine Christianity: Essays on its Setting, Sources, and Theology* (Columbia, S.C.: University of South Carolina Press, 1984) pp. 187-88.

[9]John 6:23, 68; 9:38; 11:2, 3, 12, 21, 27, 32, 34, 39; 13:6, 9, 13, 14, 25, 36, 37; 14:5, 8, 22; 20:2, 13, 18, 20, 25, 28; 21:7 (bis), 12, 15, 16, 17, 20, 21. In addition, *kurios* is translated as "master," referring at least indirectly to Jesus, in 13:16; 15:15, 20. For *kurios* as "sir," applied to someone other than Jesus, cf. 12:21; 20:15.

[10]In *Leg. All.* i. 2, 3, quoted by J. H. Bernard, *A Critical and Exegetical Commentary on the Gospel According to St. John*, Vol. I. The International Critical Commentary. (New York: Charles Scribner's Sons, 1929) p. 236.

[11]The *pericope de adultera*, 7:53-8:11, which appears at various points in John or Luke, may be omitted from consideration here on grounds of textual uncertainty. Without it, the connection between Chapters 7 and 8 is more evident.

[12]C.K. Barrett, *The Gospel According to St. John*, 2nd ed. (Philadelphia: The Westminster Press, 1978) pp. 309, 313.

[13]Rudolf Bultmann, *The Gospel of John: A Commentary* (Philadelphia: The Westminster Press, 1971) p. 165, note 1.

Although it lies beyond the scope of the present study to investigate John's use of gnostic themes and terminology, it is significant that relation analysis can touch on this issue and thus intersect with historical-critical study at this point. C.K. Barrett discusses some of the issues concerning John and gnosticism in *Essays on John* (Philadelphia: The Westminster Press, 1982) pp. 8-14, 72-74, 108.

[14]C.F.D. Moule, *An Idiom-Book of New Testament Greek* (Cambridge: Cambridge University Press, 1953) pp. 112-13 and, more generally, 106-17. Cf. also James H. Moulton, *A Grammar of New Testament Greek*, Vol. III, Syntax, by Nigel Turner (Edinburgh: T. & T. Clark, 1963) pp. 175-76, and, more generally, 172-84.

[15]Moule, *op. cit.*, pp. 112-13.

[16]Moulton (Turner), *op. cit.*, p. 175. The author also points out that a noun before a genitive may be anarthrous as a reflection of the Hebrew construct state.

[17]On 7:37b-38 cf. Barrett, *The Gospel According to St. John*, pp. 326-27.

[18]Barrett, *op. cit.*, p. 462.

[19]On the expression "I am" in John, cf. Philip B. Harner, *The "I Am" of the Fourth Gospel* (Philadelphia: Fortress Press, 1970). On the expression "I am He," cf. Philip B. Harner, *Grace and Law in Second Isaiah: "I am the Lord"* (Lewiston/Queenston: The Edwin Mellen Press, 1988).

[20]John uses the expression *pisteuo eis* for believing in Jesus in 1:12; 2:11, 23; 3:16, 18, 36; 4:39; 6:29, 35, 40; 7:5, 31, 38-39, 48; 8:30; 9:35-36; 10:42; 11:25-26, 45, 48; 12:11, 36-37, 42, 44, 46; 14:1, 12; 16:9; 17:20. Only in 12:44 and 14:1 does he use the phrase to refer to believing in God. Cf. W.F. Moulton and A.S. Geden, *A Concordance to the Greek Testament* (Edinburgh: T. & T. Clark, 1926) s.v. *pisteuo*.

[21]For Hillers' explanation of the "love of God" in Deuteronomy cf. Delbert R. Millers, *Covenant: The History of a Biblical Idea* (Baltimore: The Johns Hopkins Press, 1969) pp. 152-54. Hillers refers (p. 151) to W.L. Moran, "The Ancient Near Eastern Background of the Love of God in Deuteronomy," *Catholic Biblical Quarterly* 25 (1963) pp. 77-87.

[22]Cf. Harner, *The "I Am" of the Fourth Gospel.*

[23]Cf. Philip B. Harner, *Understanding the Lord's Prayer* (Philadelphia: Fortress Press, 1975) pp. 104-06.

[24]E.g., 1:9, 10ab; 3:17a, 19; 6:14; 9:39; 10:36; 11:9, 27; 12:25, 46; 13:1 (bis); 16:21, 28 (bis), 33a; 17:5, 11 (bis), 13, 15, 18 (bis), 24; 18:37; 21:25.

[25]8:23; 12:25; 13:1; 14:17, 19, 22, 27, 31; 15:19; 16:20, 28, 33; 17:6, 9, 11, 13, 14, 15, 16; 18:20, 36.

[26]Cf. Barrett, *The Gospel According to St. John*, p. 506.

[27]From the standpoint of historical study, J. Louis Martyn has utilized Chapter 9 as a major source for his study of the expulsion of (Jewish) Christians from the synagogue. Thus he argues that 9:22 refers to action taken under Gamaliel II at Jamnia to reword the Birkath ha-Minim with special reference to Christians. Cf. J. Louis Martyn, *History and Theology in the Fourth Gospel*, Rev. Ed. (Nashville: Abingdon, 1979) p. 61. Martyn believes that John's text presents a two-level drama, witnessing to the *einmalig* tradition about the earthly Jesus and also to the presence of Jesus as risen Lord in the events experienced by the Johannine church.

[28]Comment made by Professor J. Edward Dirks in a chapel talk at Yale Divinity School, New Haven, Connecticut, ca. 1959.

[29]The quotation is from Leland Ryken, "Formalist and Archetypal Criticism," in Clarence Walhout and Leland Ryken, eds., *Contemporary Literary Theory: A Christian Appraisal* (Grand Rapids, Michigan: William B. Eerdmans Publishing Company, 1991) p. 11.

[30]Edgar Krentz, *The Historical-Critical Method* (Philadelphia: Fortress Press, 1975) p. 44.

[31]Krentz, *op. cit.*, p. 71.

[32]Terence J. Keegan, O.P., *Interpreting the Bible: A Popular Introduction to Biblical Hermeneutics* (New York, N.Y./Mahwah, N.J.: Paulist Press, 1975) p. 76. For a history of the development of the New Criticism and an assessment of its continuing significance, see John R. Willingham, "The New Criticism: Then and Now," in *Contemporary Literary Theory*, ed. by G. Douglas Atkins and Laura Morrow (Amherst: The University of Massachusetts Press, 1989) pp. 24-41.

[33]Cf. Moore, *Literary Criticism and the Gospels*, pp. 9-13.

[34]Cf. Robert Kysar, "Johannine Metaphor--Meaning and Function: A Literary Case Study of John 10:1-8," in R. Alan Culpepper and Fernando F. Segovia, eds., *Semeia 53: The Fourth Gospel from a Literary Perspective* (Atlanta, GA: Scholars Press, 1991) pp. 81-111, especially Pp. 97-101; the quoted words are from p. 99.

[35]Kysar, *op. cit.*, p. 99.

[36]Keegan, *op. cit.*, pp. 10-11; cf. also pp. 44-45, 78-80.

[37]Peter J. Rabinowitz, "Whirl without End: Audience-Oriented Criticism," in *Contemporary Literary Theory*, ed. by G. Douglas Atkins and Laura Morrow, p. 86.

On the different types of reader-response criticism, with attention to figures such as Norman Holland, David Bleich, Jonathan Culler, Stanley Fish, Wolfgang Iser, Hans Robert Jauss, and Louise Marie Rosenblatt, cf. Michael Vander Weele, "Reader-Response Theories," in *Contemporary Literary Theory: A Christian Appraisal*, ed. by Clarence Walhout and Leland Ryken, pp. 125-48.

[38]Cf. Iser's comment, "Indeed, it is only through inevitable omissions that a story gains its dynamism. Thus whenever the flow is interrupted and we are led off in unexpected directions, the opportunity is given to us to bring into play our own faculty for establishing connections--for filling in the gaps left by the text itself." Wolfgang Iser, *The Implied Reader*, p. 280.

[39]Iser, *op. cit.*, p. 87.

[40]Iser, *op. cit.*, pp. 85, 87-88.

[41]Keegan, *op. cit.*, pp. 79-83.

[42]Keegan, *op. cit.*, pp. 86-90. For the idea that the reader is not completely autonomous, cf. also McKnight, *Post-Modern Use of the Bible*, pp. 15, 61.

[43]Keegan, *op. cit.*, p. 147.

[44]Keegan, *op. cit.*, pp. 145-59.

[45]Cf. Culpepper's comment on the narrative world in John: "The gospel claims that its world is, or at least reflects something that is, more 'real' than the world the reader has encountered previously. The text is therefore a mirror in which readers can 'see' the world in which they live. Its meaning is produced in the experience of reading the gospel and lies on this side of the text, between the reader and the text" (*Anatomy of the Fourth Gospel*, p. 5; cf. pp. 236-37).

[46]Mark W. G. Stibbe, *John as Storyteller: Narrative Criticism and the Fourth Gospel*. Society for New Testament Studies Monograph Series 73. (Cambridge, England; New York: Cambridge University Press, 1992) p. 13.

[47]Stibbe, *op. cit.*, p. 76.

[48]Cf. Johannes Beutler, "Response from a European Perspective," in R. Alan Culpepper and Fernando F. Segovia eds., *Semeia 53: The Fourth Gospel from a Literary Perspective*, pp. 191-202.

BIBLIOGRAPHY

Atkins, G. Douglas, and Laura Morrow, eds. *Contemporary Literary Theory.* Amherst: The University of Massachusetts Press, 1989.

Barrett, C.K. *Essays on John.* Philadelphia: The Westminster Press, 1982.

_____. *The Gospel According to St. John.* 2nd ed. Philadelphia: The Westminster Press, 1978.

Bernard, J.H. *A Critical and Exegetical Commentary on the Gospel According to St. John.* Vols. I, II. The International Critical Commentary. New York: Charles Scribner's Sons, 1929.

Beutler, Johannes. "Response from a European Perspective." In R. Alan Culpepper and Fernando F. Segovia, eds., *Semeia 53: The Fourth Gospel from a Literary Perspective*, pp. 191-202.

Beutler, Johannes, and Robert T. Fortna, eds. *The Shepherd Discourse of John 10 and Its Context.* Society for New Testament Studies Monograph Series 67. New York: Cambridge University Press, 1991.

Brown, Raymond E. *The Gospel According to John*, I-XII, XIII-XXI. The Anchor Bible 29, 29A. Garden City, NY: Doubleday & Company, 1966, 1970.

Bultmann, Rudolf. *The Gospel of John: A Commentary.* Philadelphia: The Westminster Press, 1971.

Carson, D.A. *The Gospel According to John.* Leicester: InterVarsity; Grand Rapids, MI: Eerdmans, 1991.

Countryman, L. William. *The Mystical Way in the Fourth Gospel: Crossing Over into God.* Philadelphia: Fortress Press, 1987.

Crosman, Inge. See Suleiman, Susan R.

Culpepper, R. Alan. *Anatomy of the Fourth Gospel: A Study in Literary Design*. Philadelphia: Fortress Press, 1983.

Culpepper, R. Alan, and Fernando F. Segovia, eds. *Semeia 53: The Fourth Gospel from a Literary Perspective*. Atlanta, GA: Scholars Press, 1991.

Duke, Paul D. *Irony in the Fourth Gospel*. Atlanta: John Knox, 1985.

Eco, Umberto. *The Limits of Interpretation*. Bloomington, Indiana: Indiana University Press, 1990.

Fortna, Robert T., and Beverly R. Gaventa, eds. *The Conversation Continues: Studies in Paul & John, In Honor of J. Louis Martyn*. Nashville: Abingdon Press, 1990.

Fortna, Robert T. See Beutler, Johannes.

Gaventa, Beverly R. See Fortna, Robert T.

Geden, A. S. See Moulton, W. F.

Hall, Vernon, Jr. *A Short History of Literary Criticism*. New York: New York University Press, 1963.

Harner, Philip B. *Grace and Law in Second Isaiah: "I am the Lord."* Lewiston/Queenston: The Edwin Mellen Press, 1988.

_____. *The "I Am" of the Fourth Gospel*. Philadelphia: Fortress Press, 1970.

_____. *Understanding the Lord's Prayer*. Philadelphia: Fortress Press, 1975.

Harrington, Daniel J., S.J. *John's Thought and Theology: An Introduction*. Good News Studies 33. Wilmington, DE: Glazier, 1990.

Hillers, Delbert R. *Covenant: The History of a Biblical Idea*. Baltimore: The Johns Hopkins Press, 1969.

Howard, Wilbert Francis. *The Fourth Gospel in Recent Criticism and Interpretation*. 4th ed., rev. by C. K. Barrett. London: The Epworth Press, 1955.

Hunter, Archibald M. *According to John: The New Look at the Fourth Gospel*. Philadelphia: The Westminster Press, 1968.

Iser, Wolfgang. *The Act of Reading: A Theory of Aesthetic Response*. Baltimore and London: The Johns Hopkins University Press, 1978.

_____. *The Implied Reader: Patterns of Communication in Prose Fiction from Bunyan to Beckett*. Baltimore and London: The Johns Hopkins University Press, 1974.

Keegan, Terence J., O.P. *Interpreting the Bible: A Popular Introduction to Biblical Hermeneutics.* New York, N.Y./Mahwah, N.J.: Paulist Press, 1985.

Krentz, Edgar. *The Historical-Critical Method.* Philadelphia: Fortress Press, 1975.

Kysar, Robert. *The Fourth Evangelist and His Gospel: An Examination of Contemporary Scholarship.* Minneapolis: Augsburg Publishing House, 1975.

_____. "Johannine Metaphor--Meaning and Function: A Literary Case Study of John 10:1-8." In R. Alan Culpepper and Fernando F. Segovia, eds., *Semeia 53: The Fourth Gospel from a Literary Perspective*, pp. 81-111.

_____. *John's Story of Jesus.* Philadelphia: Fortress Press, 1984.

Loader, William. *The Christology of the Fourth Gospel: Structure and Issues.* New York: Peter Lang Publishing, Inc., 1989.

McKnight, Edgar. *Postmodern Use of the Bible: The Emergence of Reader-Oriented Criticism.* Nashville, TN: Abingdon Press, 1988.

Martyn, J. Louis. *History and Theology in the Fourth Gospel.* Rev. ed. Nashville: Abingdon, 1979.

Moore, Stephen D. *Literary Criticism and the Gospels: The Theoretical Challenge.* New Haven: Yale University Press, 1989.

More, Sister Thomas. *"His Witness is True": John and His Interpreters.* New York: Peter Lang Publishing, Inc., 1989.

Morrow, Laura. See Atkins, G. Douglas.

Moule, C.F.D. *An Idiom-Book of New Testament Greek.* Cambridge: Cambridge University Press, 1953.

Moulton, James H. *A Grammar of New Testament Greek.* Vol. III, Syntax, by Nigel Turner. Edinburgh: T. & T. Clark, 1963.

Moulton, W.F., and A.S. Geden. *A Concordance to the Greek Testament.* Edinburgh: T. & T. Clark, 1926.

O'Day, Gail R. *Revelation in the Fourth Gospel: Narrative Mode and Theological Claim.* Philadelphia Fortress Press, 1986.

Rabinowitz, Peter J. "Whirl without End: Audience-Oriented Criticism." *In Contemporary Literary Theory*, ed. by G. Douglas Atkins and Laura Morrow, pp. 81-100.

Ryken, Leland. See Walhout, Clarence.

Segovia, Fernando F. "Towards a New Direction in Johannine Scholarship: The Fourth Gospel from a Literary Perspective." In R. Alan Culpepper and Fernando F. Segovia, eds., *Semeia 53: The Fourth Gospel from a Literary Perspective*, pp. 1-22.

Segovia, Fernando F. See Culpepper, R. Alan.

Selden, Raman. *A Reader's Guide to Contemporary Literary Theory*. Lexington, Kentucky: The University Press of Kentucky, 1985.

Sloyan, Gerard S. *What Are They Saying About John?* Mahwah, N.J.: Paulist Press, 1991.

Smith, D. Moody. *Johannine Christianity: Essays on its Setting, Sources, and Theology*. Columbia, S.C.: University of South Carolina Press, 1984.

_____. *John*. 2nd ed. Proclamation Commentaries. Philadelphia: Fortress Press, 1986.

_____. *John Among the Gospels: The Relationship in Twentieth-Century Research*. Minneapolis: Fortress Press, 1992.

Staley, Jeffrey Lloyd. *The Print's First Kiss: A Rhetorical Investigation of the Implied Reader in the Fourth Gospel*. Society of Biblical Literature Dissertation Series 82. Atlanta, GA: Scholars Press, 1988.

Staton, Shirley F., ed. *Literary Theories in Praxis*. Philadelphia: The University of Pennsylvania Press, 1987.

Stibbe, Mark W. G. *John as Storyteller: Narrative Criticism and the Fourth Gospel*. Society for New Testament Studies Monograph Series 73. Cambridge, England; New York: Cambridge University Press, 1992.

Suleiman, Susan R., and Inge Crosman, eds. *The Reader in the Text: Essays on Audience and Interpretation*. Princeton: Princeton University Press, 1980.

Tompkins, Jane P., ed. *Reader-Response Criticism: From Formalism to Post-Structuralism*. Baltimore and London: The Johns Hopkins University Press, 1980.

Turner, Nigel. See Moulton, James H.

Vander Weele, Michael. "Reader-Response Theories." In Clarence Walhout and Leland Ryken, eds., *Contemporary Literary Theory: A Christian Appraisal*, pp. 125-48.

Walhout, Clarence, and Leland Ryken. *Contemporary Literary Theory: A Christian Appraisal*. Grand Rapids, Michigan: William B. Eerdmans Publishing Company, 1991.

Wilder, Amos N. *The Bible and the Literary Critic*. Minneapolis: Augsburg Fortress, 1990.

Willingham, John R. "The New Criticism: Then and Now." In G. Douglas Atkins and Laura Morrow, eds., *Contemporary Literary Theory*, pp. 24-41.

INDEX OF SCRIPTUAL REFERENCES

DATE DUE

DATE DUE			
DEC 1 9 1994			
DEC 1 4 1996			
JUN 1 6 2002			
			Printed in USA